IRWIN ALLEN COLLECTIBLES

JOHN BUSS

First published 2023

Amberley Publishing
The Hill, Stroud
Gloucestershire, GL5 4EP

www.amberley-books.com

Copyright © John Buss, 2023

The right of John Buss to be identified as the Author of this work has been asserted in accordance with the Copyrights, Designs and Patents Act 1988.

ISBN 978 1 3981 1531 6 (print)
ISBN 978 1 3981 1532 3 (ebook)

All rights reserved. No part of this book may be reprinted or reproduced or utilised in any form or by any electronic, mechanical or other means, now known or hereafter invented, including photocopying and recording, or in any information storage or retrieval system, without the permission in writing from the Publishers.

British Library Cataloguing in Publication Data.

A catalogue record for this book is available from the British Library.

Typeset in 10pt on 13pt Celeste.
Typesetting by SJmagic DESIGN SERVICES, India.
Printed in Great Britain.

Appointed GPSR EU Representative: Easy Access System Europe Oü, 16879218
Address: Mustamäe tee 50, 10621, Tallinn, Estonia
Contact Details: gpsr.requests@easproject.com, +358 40 500 3575

Contents

Irwin Allen Collectibles 4

Land of the Giants 5

Lost in Space 35

The Time Tunnel 51

Voyage to the Bottom of the Sea 58

Acknowledgements 96

Irwin Allen Collectibles

What is the appeal to Irwin Allen's shows? Shows, which to a modern eye, despite the relatively high budgets ($250,000 an episode for *Land of the Giants*), always seemed to look cheap. Largely, this was down to the studio-bound appearance, use of stock footage, costumes, etc. The same alien costumes – amongst other things – turn up in all four of his series. Special effects work is also patchy, from the quite spectacularly convincing to some really quite awful back projection.

They were, however, new and exciting in comparison to the television science fiction that had appeared before. Allen had worked mainly in movies throughout the 1950s, ending up at 20th Century Fox, where he was to produce the feature film *Voyage to the Bottom of the Sea* in 1961. He would adapt this movie to become his first TV series in 1964, reusing many of the movies sets and costumes. Television before this was mostly dominated by westerns. Allen was amongst a small group of producers who would forge ahead and break this dominance with new and original ideas. Irwin Allen's shows themselves became a dominate force in TV science fiction throughout the sixties. He followed *Voyage* with *Lost in Space*, possibly his best-known series, before moving on to *The Time Tunnel* and his final 1960s series *Land of the Giants,* running between 1968 and 1970. A common factor shared by three of his series is the theme of a small group of people trapped in unfamiliar surroundings looking for a way home. Maybe this was the appeal: the interaction of these small groups and how they come together to form a team.

This book is an attempt to showcase a selection of just some of the multitude of different products made available for Irwin Allen's classic television series.

Land of the Giants

Land of the Giants, or maybe that should be world of giants, as this series is set upon another planet. A planet that mirrors our own society, except, everything is twelve times the size it is on Earth. The series centres on the crew and passengers aboard the *Spindrift*, Flight 612 (or 703 in the novelised version), which while on its scheduled flight between Los Angeles and London, passes through a violent atmospheric storm where a strange cloud formation is encountered. This draws the *Spindrift* into its centre and transports them to this planet of giants.

Unaware that they are no longer over their intended destination, power cells running low, Steve Burton (Gary Conway), the pilot of this ill-fated craft, unable to communicate with London, takes them in for an emergency landing. Landing in dense fog and still unable to obtain any communication both Steve and his co-pilot, Dan Erickson (Don Marshall), decide to investigate outside. It is here that they discover things are no longer quite how they should be, though it is never made clear in this first episode whether they are no longer on Earth, or whether they may have been reduced in size somehow by the cloud formation.

Venturing outside into the fog, they are nearly run over by an approaching giant car, before running back to the relative safety of the *Spindrift*. An attempted emergency take-off is hindered by the arrival of a 'small' boy who picks up the craft to examine it, peering curiously in at the windows before its straining engines summon enough power to break free. However, with low power reserves the *Spindrift* soon has to land, leaving our group trapped in this strange *Land of the Giants*.

The other members of this group are Betty Hamilton (Heather Young), their stewardess, whilst the passengers consisted of Mark Wilson (Don Matheson), an engineer/businessman; Commander Fitzhugh (Kurt Kasnar), a navy officer of some description, who appears to be wanted by the police in connection with the theft of $1 million, the police apparently awaiting his arrival in London; Valerie Scott (Denna Lund), a socialite (whose only contribution to the series seems to be the possession of a fine pair of lungs); and the youngest member of the group was Barry Lockridge (Stefan Arngrim), an orphan from a military family on his way to live with relatives, and his dog Chipper.

During the series run of fifty-one episodes, made to the American one-hour format (so, in plain English, fifty minutes), the group were pitted against many different perils from all the expected sources, ranging from giant cats to experimenting scientists.

As with many series, this show now seems dated largely due to the unfortunate habit producers have of setting them in the near future and specifying a year – 1983 in this case.

Products normally will have the copyright details '© Kent Productions – 20th Century Fox Film Corporation' upon them.

Books
Three paperback books, all written by Murray Leinster, were published by Pyramid Books in the USA at an original price of 60 cents. The first was simply *Land of the Giants* published

in September of 1968. The second was *Land of the Giants 2: The Hot Spot* published in April of 1969, followed by *Land of the Giants 3: Unknown Danger*.

One other book was published in the USA, which was *Flight of Fear* by Carl Henry Rathjen, released by Whitman as a hardback in 1969. This title also appears to be the only *Land of the Giants* books to have seen publication in Japan, being published by Kadokawa Shoten in 1983.

In the UK, the first two of the Pyramid titles saw publication by World Distributors, the first, now titled *Land of the Giants: The Trap*, was followed by *Land of the Giants: The Hot Spot*. The third and fourth books published in the UK run were by James Bradwell. They were *Land of the Giants: Slingshot for David* and, the last book in the UK series, *Land of the Giants: The Mean City*. All four books in the series were published in 1969, having a cover price of 3s 6d. The World Distributors titles also saw release in Australia, South Africa, Canada and New Zealand.

The three American Murray Leinster titles saw release in Germany. The first one became *Im Land der Giganten*, published by Moewig in 1969 and translated by Brigitte Kraus. The second, *Land of the Giants: The Hot Spot*, became *Die Irrfahrten der 'Spindrift'*, this time published by Ullstein in 1972. The third, *Land of the Giants: Unknown Danger*, became *Im Reich der Giganten*, again published by Ullstein, in 1973.

Land of the Giants 3: Unknown Danger appears to be the only title printed in Portuguese, published by Livros do Brasil in 1970 as *Plataforma especial*.

USA Pyramid Books No. 1 and No. 2: *The Hot Spot*.

Whitman *Flight of Fear* hardback showing a wraparound cover illustration.

Above left: USA Pyramid Books No. 3: *Unknown Danger*.

Above right: Japanese paperback. (Bernard Dunne)

UK paperbacks *The Hot Spot* and *The Trap*.

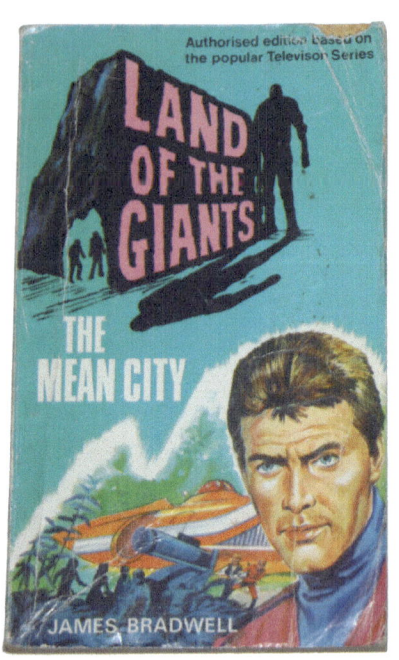
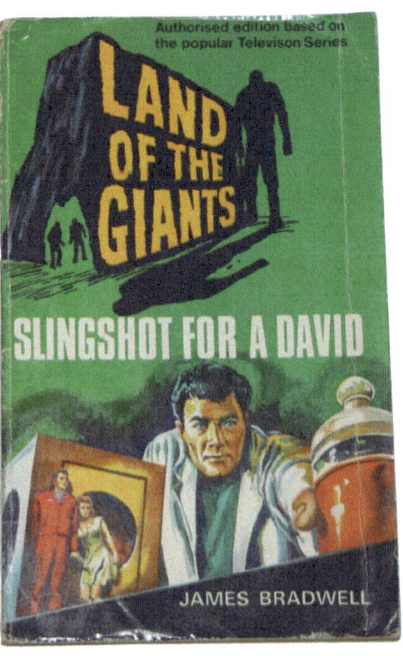

UK paperbacks *The Mean City* and *Slingshot for a David*.

Above left: German paperback *Im Land der Giganten*. (Bernard Dunne)

Above right: German paperback *Die Irrfahrten der 'Spindrift'*. (Bernard Dunne)

Right: German paperback *Im Reich der Giganten*. (Bernard Dunne)

Hardback books were published in Spain under the title *Tierra De Gigantes: El Pais De Los Gigantes* by the publishers Editorial Bruguera. S. A. in 1971, with a second also just called *Tierra De Gigantes: El Pais De Los Gigantes* in 1972. Both books contained 160 illustrations. No details for either writer or original title are presented inside either, so it has not been possible to ascertain whether these are translations of other titles or completely new stories.

Above left: Spanish book *Tierra de Gigantes*. (Bernard Dunne)

Above right: Spanish book *Prisioneros en el pais de los Gigantes*. (Bernard Dunne)

Left: UK Annual 1969.

In the UK World Distributors Ltd produced two hardback annuals for the series. The first, published in 1969 with a publication price of 12s 6d, had a photographic cover. It contained a mix of stories, features and puzzles. The second annual, published in 1970, had an illustrated cover of a giant cat chasing crewmembers of the *Spindrift*. This contained a similar mix of contents to the first annual.

An annual-sized Television Picture Story Book was also published in the UK in 1969. This was released by PBS Publishing at a price of 4s 11d and its contents consisted mostly of reprints from the Gold Key comics.

Right: UK Annual 1970.

Below left: UK Television Picture Story Book.

Below right: USA Whitman Coloring Book.

A colouring book was published in the USA by Whitman in 1969. This contained illustrations by Jason Studios. In the UK both a colouring book and a sticker fun book were produced by World Distributors in 1969, but it appears that these may have been very limited test releases not seeing large distribution, so these are very rare to find.

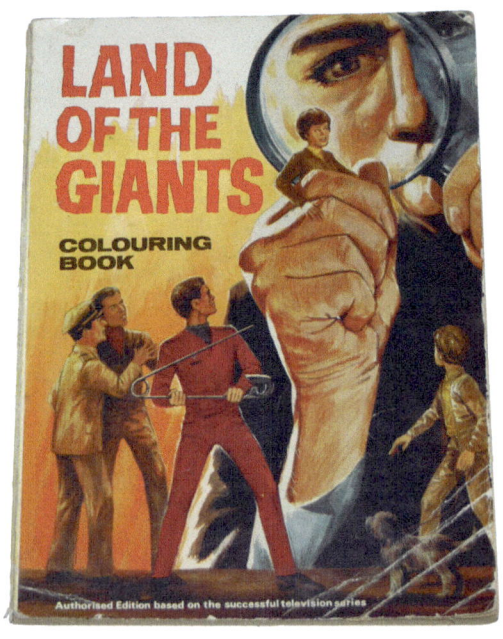

Above left: UK Colouring Book.

Above right: Sticker Fun Book. (Paul Gleave)

Joe 90: Top Secret Comic Annual, 1969.

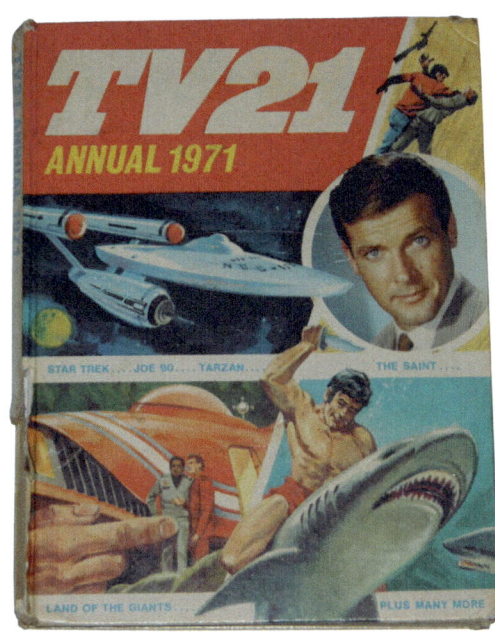

TV21 Annual 1971.

At least two other UK children's annuals contained *Land of the Giants*. The first was the *Joe 90: Top Secret* annual for 1969, published by City Magazines Ltd at a price of 12s 6d. This included two strip stories based on the series. The second was the 1971 *TV21* annual, which included both a text story, Dangerous Line, and two strip stories, Soldiers of Doom and The Giant Maker. A small illustration of the series also appeared on the cover.

Toys

Aurora produced two model kits based on the series. The first is a diorama of three members of the *Spindrift* crew facing off against a giant diamond backed rattlesnake that was produced in 1968, and sold for $1.50. The second, produced in 1969, featured the *Spindrift* aircraft. This kit, produced at approximately 1/64 scale, featured a removable top to the ship revealing a detailed interior showing the controls, cabin, etc. The first issue of this kit featured a clear plastic dome and embossed G on its side, while the 1975 reissue had a red transparent dome and the G was now a transfer, not embossed.

Midori in Japan also released a model kit of the *Spindrift* in 1969. It was produced in orange plastic, with an electric motor and wheels so the assembled model could move around the floor.

Colorforms produced a cartoon kit in 1968, consisting of thin plastic shapes that could be stuck upon a colourful background. Colorforms produced many of different cartoon kits, featuring different popular TV series of the time.

Chemtoy produced a small movie viewer in 1969 priced at 59 cents. This consisted of a small plastic generic viewer within which you could insert one of the two small filmstrips included. A small winder on the side enabled the film to pass through for viewing, which was achieved by holding up to the light and looking through the small eyepiece. Some backing cards have the logo for and credit production to K-Kids rather than Chemtoy.

Advert and Aurora snake model kit. (Norman Fisher)

   Ideal introduced a board game based upon the series in 1968. The illustrated box showed the *Spindrift* crew fending off a giant cat with a pencil. Intended for a maximum of four people, play takes the form of a scavenger hunt. Players have to obtain pieces of equipment and return to the *Spindrift* avoiding capture by giants. The first player to return with all the required items wins.

   The only jigsaw that appears to have been produced for the series was a large, 20-inch-diameter round puzzle featuring Steve, Valerie, Barry and Chipper being menaced by a giant cat. This was produced by Whitman in 1968.

Box for Aurora *Spindrift* kit.

Aurora *Spindrift* reissue 1975. (Vectis)

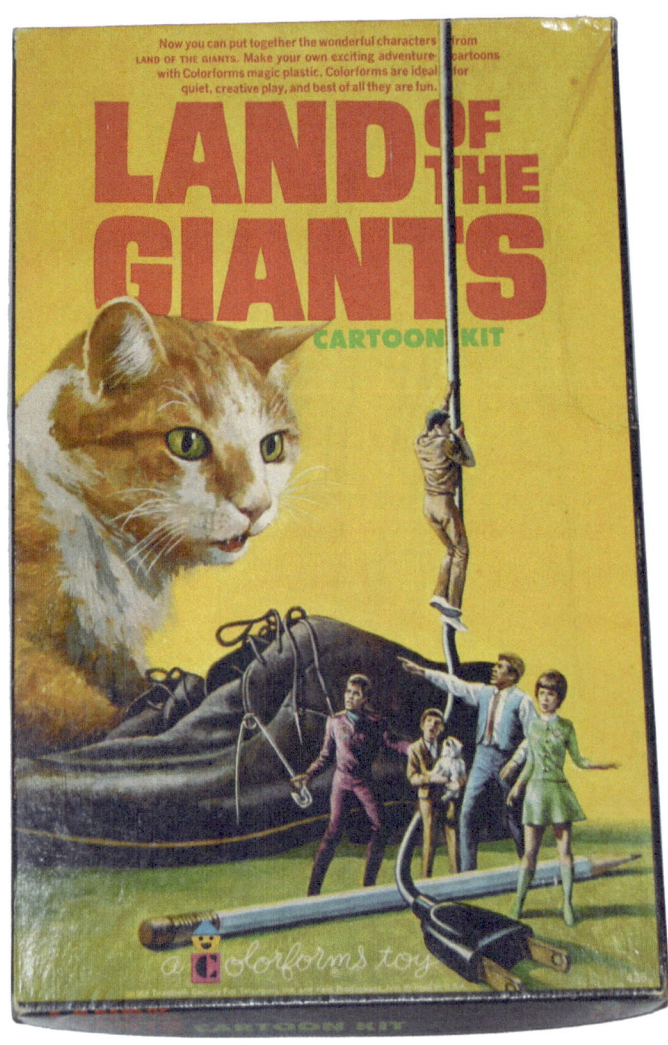

Left: Colorforms cartoon kit.

Below: Colorforms cartoon kit.

Above left: Chemtoy movie viewer.

Above right: Ideal board game.

Above left: Round jigsaw.

Above right: *Spindrift* toothpick craft kit.

    Remco Industries appear to have been by far the largest producer of tie-in products for the show, producing at least seven. One was the Spindrift Toothpick Craft Set. This consisted of several printed card sections of the ship, which were joined together by toothpicks, packs of which were included within the kit.

    Another Remco product was the Space Sled, which was a repurposed version of their Supercar model, now in blue and white plastic but originally in red. It came complete with a moulded figure of what was clearly Mike Mercury still at the controls. This battery-operated toy could be programmed to move around in one of several pre-set courses by the inserting of one of several different round discs into a compartment behind the driver. Some examples have a blue base with white upper, while other examples have the colours reversed – white base with blue top.

Remco space sled. (Robert Vanderpool)

Spaceship control panel. (Robert Vanderpool)

A battery-operated spaceship control panel with switches and steering wheel representing the controls to the *Spindrift* was produced by Remco. This toy appears to have started out in the 1950s as Remco's Firebird 99 Toy Car dashboard, which was repurposed with new decals and colour scheme to become the spaceship control panel. This same product, again with a different colour scheme, also saw issue as a Working Black Beauty Dashboard from the *Green Hornet*.

Remco was also responsible for a Shoot'n Stick rifle. This child's hard plastic rifle, approximately 29 inches long, came with a 9 × 9.25 inch fabric-covered target, topped with a logo-shaped header, that Velcro-tipped darts could be fired at, six of which were included. The rifle had a spring-loaded firing mechanism and a flip-up simulated targeting sight. The shoulder stock also displayed a sticker with the show's logo upon it.

Again from Remco was a motorised flying rocket. This is more of a battery-operated aircraft than a rocket, which flies attached to the end of a tether, the batteries contained in a hand pack with power travelling up the tether to the small electric motor contained within the craft.

A signal ray space gun was yet another product produced for the series – once again an example of Remco reusing existing products in a new guise. This gun had previously been used as a *Lost in Space* product. The *Land of the Giants* version is black and red plastic, while the *Lost in Space* version is chromed silver and red.

Shoot'n Stick Target Rifle. (Robert Vanderpool)

Left: Flying rocket, Remco. (Robert Vanderpool)

Below: Signal ray gun. (Robert Vanderpool)

Walkie talkies. (Robert Vanderpool)

Also having previously been a different product were the *Land of the Giants* walkie talkies set, which also appeared as *Star Trek* walkie talkies. A much cheaper product produced by Remco was the *Land of the Giants* frisbee. A cheap plastic frisbee marketed as a flying saucer, the plastic disc came shrink wrapped on a generic printed backing card, while the disc had a printed-paper label on its centre with graphics and the legend flying spaceship *Spindrift*. All of these Remco products were produced in 1968 and only ever released in the USA.

Ben Cooper produced at least five different Halloween costumes based upon *Land of the Giants*. All costumes known about came in generic boxes with the only details being the title of the show and the costumes name printed on the box end. The most common appears to be the Giant Professor. The one-piece costume with a mask has a printed orange top with a wide printed blue and yellow tie, with attached blue sleeves and trouser bottoms. Also printed on the top were three of the cast climbing from the printed-on pockets, while the mask depicts a bearded face. Two box styles have been seen for this costume: one has a fully cut-out face-shaped window, while the window on the other version only has the bottom half of the face cut out. Another version of this costume has been seen containing a cyclops-style mask.

Ben Cooper costume giant mask and rare alternative costume. (Robert Vanderpool)

Above: Ben Cooper costume cyclops. (Robert Vanderpool)

Left: Ben Cooper costume giant mask and costume standard issue. (Norman Fisher)

Above: Ben Cooper costume cat. (Robert Vanderpool)

Right: Ben Cooper costume witch. (Robert Vanderpool)

The second costume depicts a giant witch. This costume, a printed dress, has four of the characters from the show fleeing a giant cat printed on its front, while the mask included depicts the face of a wizened old hag.

A third costume is a giant cat. This costume, which came with a cat mask, shows three of the little people on its chest attacking it with a giant safety pin.

The next two costumes feature characters from the series: Steve Burton and Dan Erikson. The Steve Burton costume is a representation of the red flight uniform worn by the character in the series with a mask of the actor's face. The Dan Erikson costume likewise is a representation of the character's costume in the series, though the top in this case is blue. As with the Steve Burton costume, this came with a mask of the actor's face.

Originally produced by Sawyers, View-Master was first launched as a three-dimensional viewing system in 1939. The system consists of reels that each contain seven pairs of images, which, when combined using the special viewer, would give you a 3D image. Originally sets were primarily aimed at tourists and they would feature places of interest, but during the 1950s the company began to move into producing reels based on television shows and films, which ultimately included sets for all four of Irwin Allen's TV series. At some point during 1966 Sawyers were taken over by the General Aniline & Film (GAF) Corporation and the *Land of the Giants* set was produced during this later period of the

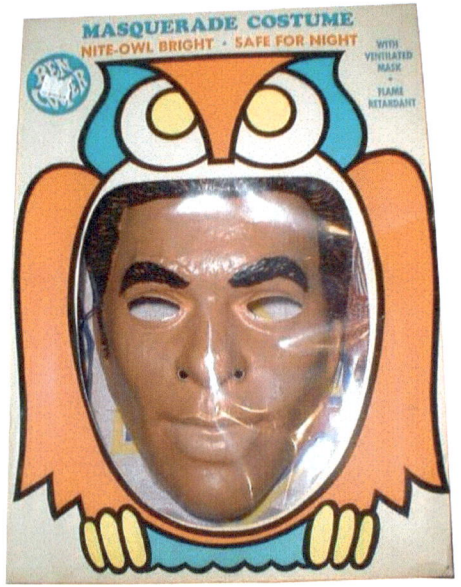

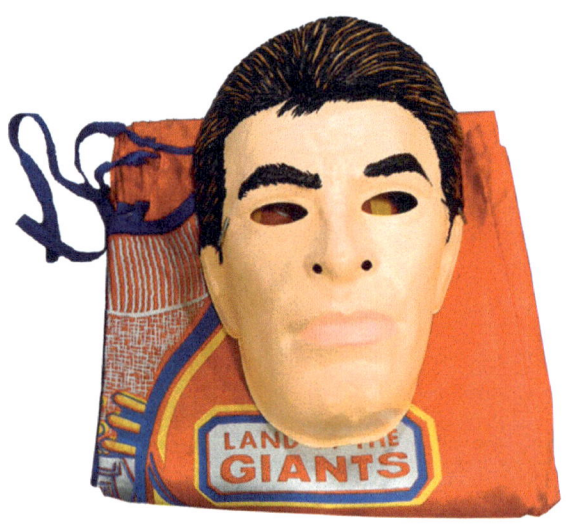

Above: Ben Cooper costumes of Dan and Steve. (Robert Vanderpool)

Left: Reel set

company's history under the GAF brand name in 1968. As was the norm for reel sets, it consisted of three reels, giving a total of twenty-one stereo photographs. A sixteen-page booklet of the story was also included. The set number was B494 and it was based on the opening episode of the series 'The Crash'.

The firm Bantamlite appear to have produced several different flashlights for the series in 1968. The first is a largish whistle flashlight in blue plastic. Then there was the wrist flashlight, which was shaped like an oversized wristwatch and could be flashed in three different colours, again produced in a blue plastic with a blue vinyl strap. Then there was a basic rectangular flashlight produced in a red plastic. Items came individually bubble wrapped on similar looking header cards. Each also had a sticker of the show's logo upon the product's side.

Watkins Strathmore produced what they called a Magic Slate. This drawing toy allowed the user to draw upon a waxed board covered with a thin plastic sheet using a supplied plastic stylus. Once the drawing was finished the plastic sheet when pulled upwards would wipe the slate clean enabling a fresh drawing to be made. This product was original sold for 29 cents in 1968.

A deluxe numbered pencil colouring set was produced by Hasbro in 1969, containing ten images for colouring along with twelve colour pencils. Hasbro also produced an oil painting by numbers set including ten pots of oil paint, a brush and two canvases. Another Hasbro product was a target game featuring a metal target of a giant cat, with suction-tipped darts.

 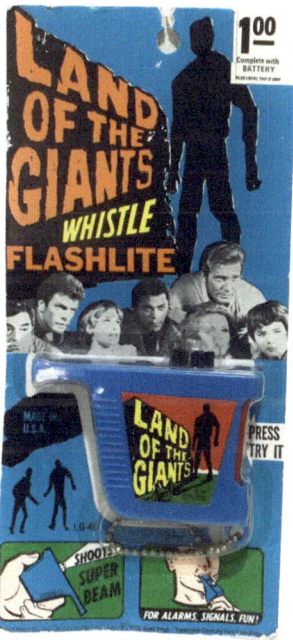 

Above left: Wrist flashlight. (Robert Vanderpool)

Above middle: Whistle flashlight. (Norman Fisher)

Above right: Magic slate. (Norman Fisher)

Above: Deluxe Numbered Pencil Colouring Set. (Robert Vanderpool)

Left: Oil Painting by Numbers. (Robert Vanderpool)

Magazines and Comics

Gold Key produced five issues of a *Land of the Giants* comic, all issued at a publication price of 15 cents. The first issue published in November 1968 contained the story 'The Mini-Criminals', with issue two in January 1969 containing 'Countdown to Escape'. Issue three from March 1969 featured the story 'Giant Damsel in Distress', while the following issue, June 1969, contained 'Safari in Giant Land'. The final issue published in September 1969 contained 'Operation Mini-Surgeon'. Artwork in these comics was by Tom Gill. At least the first issue saw translation and release in the Netherlands, being published by Classics Nederland N.V. It appears all five issues saw publication in Mexico by Domingos Alegres, as *Tierra de Gigantes*.

Above left: Gold Key comic No. 1.

Above right: Gold Key comic No. 2.

Right: Gold Key comic No. 3.

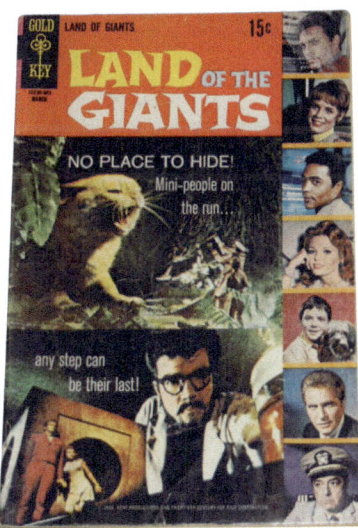

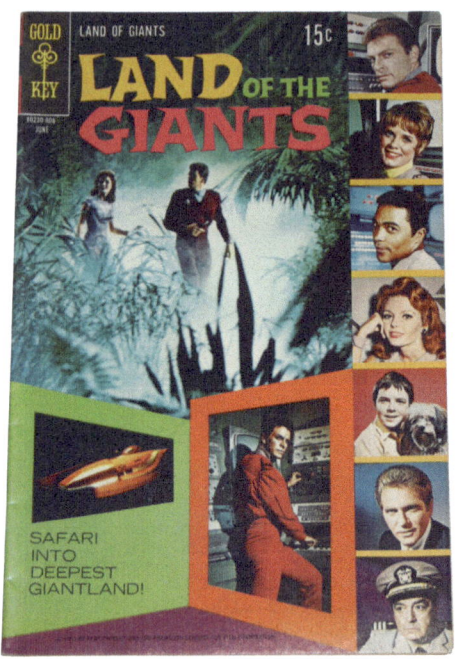 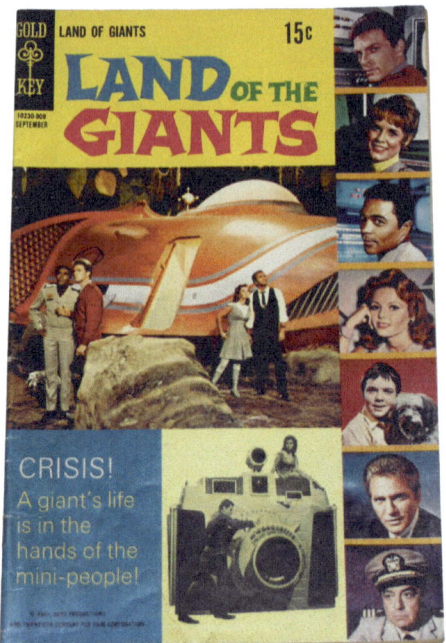

Above left: Gold Key comic No. 4.

Above right: Gold Key comic No. 5.

Above left: Dutch comic. (Remco Admiraal)

Above right: Mexican comic. (Bernard Dunne)

In the UK, *Land of the Giants* featured as a regular strip in the relatively short-lived *Joe 90: Top Secret* comic published by City Magazines at a price of 8*d* per issue. The show featured in all thirty-four issues of the comic, the first issue of which appeared on 18 January 1969. The series would feature upon the front cover of many of the comics' issues. When *Joe 90: Top Secret* came to an end the strip transferred into the new *TV21 and Joe 90* comic also from City Magazines. The first issue appeared on 27 September 1969.

TV Century 21 comic, also published by City Magazines, carried a half-page feature in issue 209, cover date 18 January 1969, about Gary Conway, promoting the series in the new *Joe 90: Top Secret* comic which had begun publication that week.

Mad Magazine would satirise the series in issue 130, cover dated October 1969, with this appearing in issue 95 of the UK edition.

Joe 90 Top Secret comic.

TV21 and Joe 90 comic.

The American listings magazine *TV Guide,* cover dated 25–31 January 1969, featured the series upon its front cover, with a photograph of Deanna Lund and Gary Conway trapped in a giant glass beaker. This issue also featured a four-page article on the show's star Gary Conway, entitled 'How's life among the Giants these days?'

Other USA TV listings magazines also carried cover photographs of the series including *Glendale News-Press TV Week* 14–20 September 1968, *Chicago Sunday Times TV Prevue* 22–28 September 1968, *St Louis Post-Dispatch TV Magazine* 29 September–5 October 1968, *The News American Weekly Magazine TV Channels* 3–9 November 1968, *Detroit Free Press TV Channels* 3–9 November 1968, *Los Angeles Times TV Times* 3–9 November 1968, *The Cleveland Press TV Showtime* 8–15 November 1968, *Boston Sunday Advertiser TVue* 10–16 November 1968, *Wisconsin TV Times* 1968, *Rocky Mountain News TV Dial* 22 June 1969, *Sunday Herald Traveler TV Magazine* 27 July–2 August 1969, *Los Angeles Herald-Examiner TV Weekly* 27 July–2 August 1969, *The Minneapolis Tribune TV Week* 25–31 January 1970, *Chicago Daily News TV* 28 February–7 March 1970.

In Canada the series featured on the cover of several TV listings magazines including *The Gazette TV Times* for Montreal 11–17 April 1970, *The Windsor Star TV Times* 11–17 April 1970 and *TV Hebdo* 11–17 October 1969.

It also appeared on the cover of a Mexican *TV Tele Guia* 4–11 October 1973.

One other notable issue is the *TV Guide* for 25–31 October 1969, which included an interview with Kurt Kasznar entitled 'He acted his way out of a paperback'.

Above left: USA TV guide.

Above right: Cleveland Press *TV Showtime*. (Norman Fisher)

Trading Cards and Miscellaneous

A set of fifty-five colour photographic cards sized approximately 55 mm × 88 mm were issued with bubblegum in 1969 by the UK firm A&BC Gum. The first forty-four cards told a story on the back while the remaining cards formed a small jigsaw. The original price per a pack of gum was 3*d*. While a few test shot wrappers have appeared for an American release of the set by Topps Chewing Gum, it appears the set never saw a full release in the USA.

Above: A&BC Gum trading cards and wrapper.

Right: Topps Gum test wrapper. (Norman Fisher)

Phoenix candy boxes. (Robert Vanderpool)

In the USA the Phoenix Candy Co. Inc. released boxes of candy in two sizes: a 0.375-oz sized box or a slightly larger 0.5-oz box. The *Land of the Giants* logos on the smaller boxes are printed in just yellow and black, while the larger boxes had the addition of red to the logo. These boxes of candy also included, dependent on box size, either one or two cheap plastic toys. Box flaps also featured a special offer, whereby if two box flaps and 50 cents were sent off to Phoenix they could obtain an ID bracelet.

20th Century Fox Television produced several interesting pieces to promote their shows such as ashtrays, china cups and glasses. These items include the Fox logo and series logos for various shows the studio had in production at the time, several of which have been seen including the logos for the various Irwin Allen series. These were promotional items that Fox would give to writers, directors, etc. ABC Television, upon which *Land of the Giants* was shown, did also produce some promotional items for giving to the general public such as a 3.5-inch button badge promoting the series.

Scrubbletoys Inc. produced bubble bath contained within an 11.5-oz bottle in the shape of a large pen. This came with an outer card box. There is very little to show that this related to the TV series as no logos or images from the series are used upon any of the packaging. Just *Land of the Giants* is written in small print on the box's front, then upon the box's side '©1969 Kent Productions'.

Aladdin Industries produced a tin lunchbox with a plastic thermos flask in 1968. The litho-printed lunchbox featured images on both sides and around the edge. The cast being

Bubble bath pen.

chased or menaced by a giant cat seems to have been a popular theme – several of the products produced for this series featured this motif. The designers of this lunchbox opted for a similar illustration upon one side of this product. The other side featured several of the crew stood in the hand of a giant. While the images are printed, both sides of the lunchbox are also embossed to make the images stand out. Around the edges are more illustrations featuring the *Spindrift* and its crew in various situations. The plastic thermos that came with this features similarly themed images, though slightly cruder in execution, to the lunchbox.

In Japan, Midori appear to have produced sketchbooks with *Land of the Giants* covers. At least two different covers were produced for these simple drawing pads.

Above left: Lunchbox side A.

Above right: Thermos.

Left: Lunchbox side B.

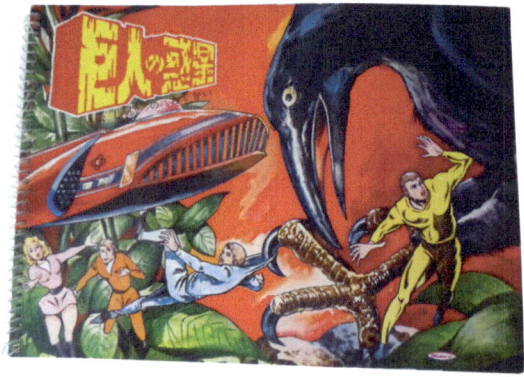

Sketchpad. (Bernard Dunne)

Lost in Space

Possibly the best known of Irwin Allen's television series is his 1965 offering, *Lost in Space*. The first series (made in black and white) introduced us to the Robinson family, who, after having been selected from over 2 million volunteers, were to be the first family launched into space in the year 1997. Chosen because of their combination of scientific achievement, emotional stability and resourcefulness, their mission was a five-and-a-half-year journey to colonise a planet in the distant Alpha Centuri system aboard the ill-fated *Jupiter 2*. Dr John Robinson (Guy Williams) was in charge with his wife, Maureen (June Lockhart), and their three children, Will (Billy Mumy), Penny (Angela Cartwright) and Judy (Marta Kristen). The other cast regulars were Mark Goddard as Don West, the *Jupiter 2*'s pilot and navigator, and Jonathan Harris, who played the treacherous Dr Zachary Smith.

Dr Smith had crept aboard the *Jupiter 2* with the intention of sabotaging the Robot (the final member of the regular line up, which contrary to popular myth was not Robby the Robot from *Forbidden Planet*, a myth perpetrated by many in the UK including BBC TV's *Telly Addicts* quiz programme). Unfortunately for Dr Smith, he became unwittingly stranded aboard upon the spacecraft's take off, his sabotage causing the *Jupiter 2* to veer off-course and crash-land on the first of many uncharted planets, causing them to become lost in space.

A total of eighty-three episodes were made, with the final colour series becoming increasingly silly, with its combination of strange, unbelievable monsters, poor scripts and the general cheapness of appearance that came from a studio-bound series. Also, the family just became too nauseatingly 'cute' in its togetherness. Of the four series to be covered in this book, this is the only one thus far to have seen reboots. Firstly a feature film version appeared in 1998, then more recently three seasons of a new TV series were made for the streaming service Netflix. Only items relating to the original 1960s TV show have been included.

Products will normally have the copyright details '© Space Productions' on them.

Books

The series original run saw only one paperback novel produced, *Lost in Space* by Dave van Arnam and Ron Archer, which was published by Pyramid Books in the USA in 1967 at a price of 60 cents. It also saw publication in Spanish, being published by Editorial Diana as *Perdidos en el espacio*, and in Japan, both in 1969.

A pad of paper was produced with a colour photo cover of June Lockhart in her role from the series in the mid-sixties, sold for 25 cents. It is probable that this product was not licensed as there are no copyright or manufacturer's details upon it.

World Distributors in the UK produced three books, tenuously linked to the series. First was the *Space Family Robinson: An All Colour Comic Album No. 1* published in 1965, which is mostly reprints from the Gold Key comics. Then in 1966 a *Space Family Robinson Annual* was produced, which contained both Gold Key reprints and original text stories based on the comics. In 1967, they again produced an annual, which contained a similar mix of

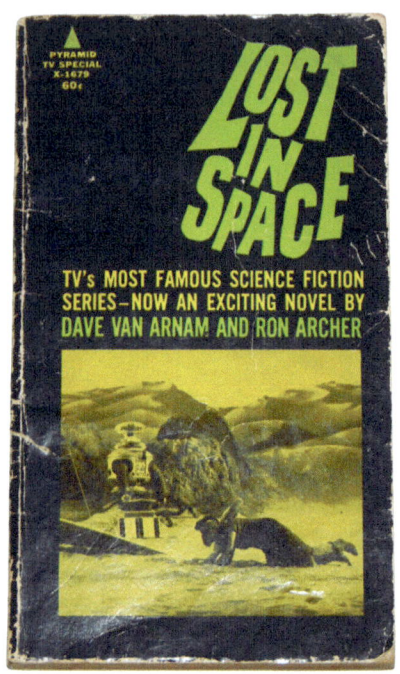

Above left: USA *Lost in Space* novel.

Above right: June Lockhart notebook.

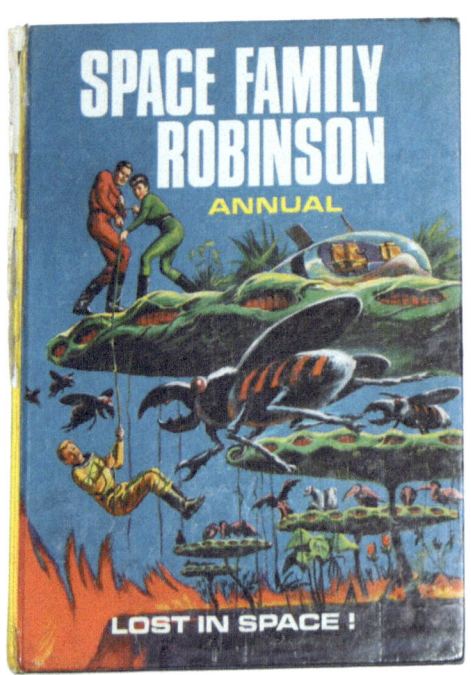

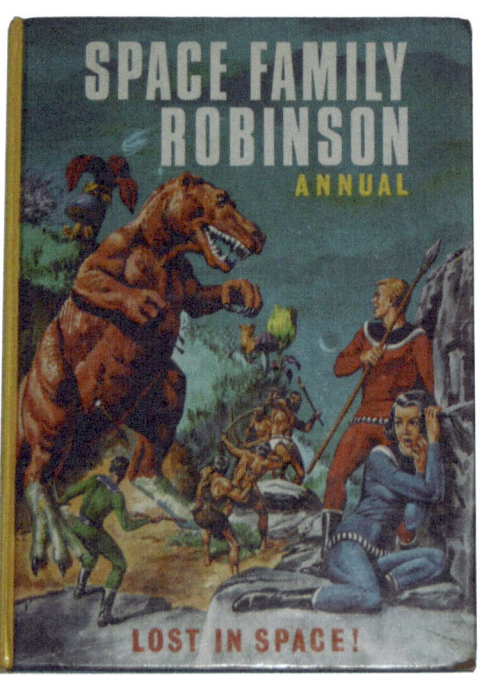

Above left: *Space Family Robinson* Annual 1966.

Above right: *Space Family Robinson* Annual 1967.

Purnell Television Stars 1966.

contents. The reason why these are only tenuously linked is looked at in more detail while discussing the original Gold Key comics.

The Purnell-published *Television Stars* book for 1966 featured a full-page photograph of the show's cast, though no other features or details for the show are included.

Toys

Well known in the USA for producing both board games and jigsaw puzzles, Milton Bradley produced both for the series in 1965. The board game playing board depicts a planet's terrain with the *Jupiter 2* in one corner and the *Chariot* in the opposite corner diagonally. In the centre of the board is an illustration of a cyclops. Very much a game of luck rather than skill, two to four players compete to be the first to cross over the hazardous planet depicted upon the board. A spinner is used in the game, which may send players off in random directions and even further away from their objective. The image used on the illustrated box lid was also used by Milton Bradley as a frame tray jigsaw. This depicted the Robinson family running away from the *Chariot*, which is being attacked by a giant cyclops. The second Milton Bradley frame puzzle shows the *Jupiter 2* in flight with the cyclops holding the *Chariot* above his head while two of the crew with jetpacks attack it. Both puzzles that have been seen contained thirty-five pieces and were approximately 10 × 14 inches in size.

Milton Bradley board game.

A frame puzzle was also produced in Japan in 1966. This came bagged on a header card and shows the Robinson family with Dr Smith, the Robot and the *Chariot*.

Remco Industries were responsible for several products relating to the series including the 3D Action Fun Game. Produced in 1966, this was a board game played across several raised cardboard levels, players swapping levels dependent on where their piece had

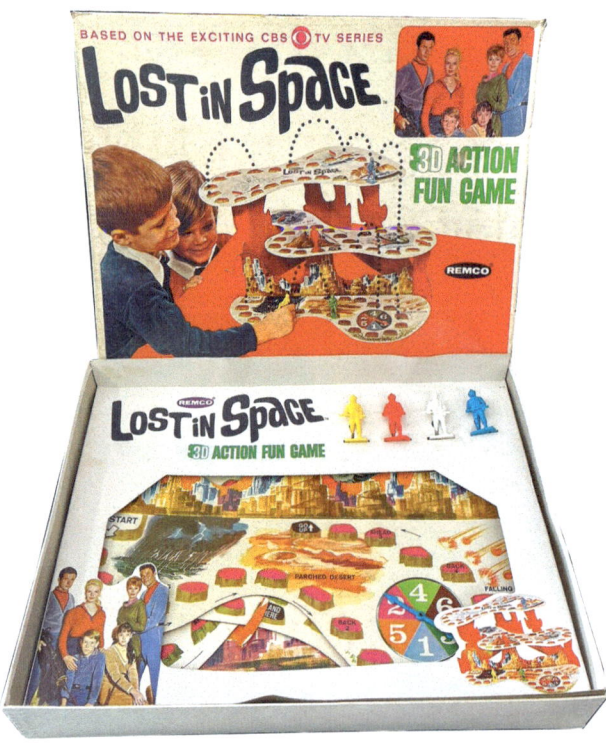

3D Action Fun Game. (Robert Vanderpool)

landed. The assembled board has the appearance of rocky outcrops that up to four players would travel across, the winner being the first to arrive at the take-off space. Play was controlled by a spinner built into the board's base level.

The most popular of Remco's products for the series by far must have been the 12-inch-tall, battery-operated model of the show's true star, the Robot. First produced in 1965, this had several features: the model's motor could propel the Robot forward and operate a light in its head, while levers upon its back enabled some basic movement of its arms. Mostly of plastic construction, it has been seen in several different colour variations. Some have a black body and base with red arms and legs. It has also been seen with these colours reversed or a blue plastic being used instead of black. Some were produced entirely in the one colour. The Robot base has stickers attached proclaiming 'Lost in Space' and showing the Robot's tracks.

A version of the Robot was also produced and sold in Mexico by the firm Ledy as 'El Robot Parlante' in 1971. Very similar in appearance to the Remco version but without control levers protruding from its back, this Mexican version also included an electronic voice box.

Another of Remco's products for the series in 1966 was the Space Helmet, which saw two different releases, either boxed on its own, or in combination with the Signal Ray Gun. The Signal Ray Gun, though released in several guises, does not appear to have been released independently with *Lost in Space* branding.

Remco robot. (Vectis)

Above left: Helmet. (Robert Vanderpool)

Above right: Helmet and ray gun set.

Mattel released a Switch and Go set in 1966, which featured both the *Jupiter 2* and *Chariot*. The *Jupiter 2* really only acted as a garage for the battery-powered *Chariot*, which ran along a plastic tube track. Switches could be placed at areas around the track, which when activated by the air pump, controlled the route the vehicle would take. Included in the set were plastic figures of the cast along with a robot, which could be towed by the *Chariot*. Several other versions of this toy appeared including one for *Batman*. The same year Mattel produced the Roto Jet Gun. This amazing weapon could be assembled in several different combinations and could fire discs that were provided with it.

A board game for the series seems to have appeared in Greece where the series was called Χαμένοι ετα Αιαιτημα, having been produced by the firm Remoundo. There appears to be several different versions. The lid of what is believed to be the first 1960s issue shows a planet landscape with a landing module of some sort having landed in a crater. A colour photograph showing Dr Smith is on the right of the lid. The next issue from the 1970s has a different landscape and illustrations of the cast's faces upon the lid. The game also appeared as part of a games compendium in the eighties, which also included a *Mission Impossible* game. The playing board for all three versions appears to be the same, showing an illustrated planet landscape with black and white photos of the crew at various places on the board.

A Halloween costume was produced by Ben Cooper in 1965, consisting of a silver one-piece suit with a printed belt and ray gun. On the top left the *Jupiter 2* is shown in flight. This came with a Nasa face mask. Four different styles of generic box have been seen for this costume, as well as two different styles of mask.

Switch and Go set.
(Norman Fisher)

Roto Jet Gun sales
sheet.

Above: Greek board game. (Robert Vanderpool)

Left: Halloween costume showing the two different mask types. (Robert Vanderpool)

The 1965 View-Master reel set for *Lost in Space* was based on the episode 'Condemned of Space'. As was the norm, the set consisted of three reels, giving a total of twenty-one stereo photographs, and a sixteen-page story booklet was included. The first issues of this set, B482, have a small triangular section in the top left corner (almost like the page of a book turning) proclaiming 'Featuring 16 page story booklet illustrated in colour'. A second edition appeared after GAF took over production. The set essentially remained the same, the GAF logo now replacing the Sawyers one. A third issue took place under GAF, which saw the packaging change. Gone is the triangular page turn in the top corner and there is now a top banner in white and orange. This is by far the rarest version of the set.

Tru-Vue Magic Eyes, another 3D system owned by GAF, would also issue a story set, featuring the same images upon its cards as were featured in the View-Master set.

View-Master reel set.

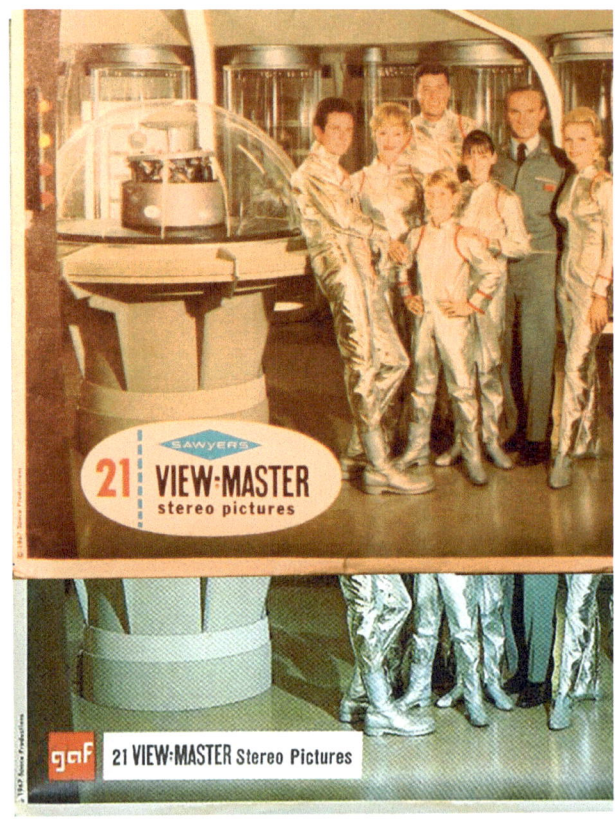

Sawyers/GAF packets comparison. (Norman Fisher)

Model kits for the series were a must, and once again Aurora stepped in to produce several kits based on the series, starting with a diorama showing the crew of the *Jupiter 2* facing off against a giant cyclops. This kit, Aurora 419, sold for around 95 cents and proved popular enough that just over a year later Aurora would issue a second kit for the show. Effectively a deluxe version of the previous diorama, Aurora 420 saw the kit produced with an expanded base and the addition of the *Chariot*, as well as a price increase to $1.98. It would also see issues for Aurora's customer service department. As quite often with the two kits being produced side by side, many would go out of the factory with the wrong instructions. The third and final *Lost in Space* model from Aurora, released in 1968, was an approximately 1/11 scale model of the Robot priced at $1.

The series proved to be extremely popular overseas and particularly in Japan, where Marusan would produce several items for the series, including what are quite possibly some of the rarest items for the show. A series of action dolls produced by the firm in 1966 featured all seven of the cast, not including the Robot, issued in card boxes with plastic tubes similar to the 'freezing' tubes on the *Jupiter 2*. As well as these figures, Marusan also produced motorised model kits of both the *Jupiter 2* and the *Chariot*.

Japan also had its own board game and a card game produced by Koide Shinkosha, who also produced decks of playing cards. Two different packs of cards appear to have been produced. One deck has illustrations of Will and the Robot on the back, with the joker being an illustration of the Robot. The other pack features an image of John and Penny Robinson on the back while the joker is Dr Smith.

Above left: Aurora kit cyclops and *Chariot* advert.

Above right: Marusan *Chariot* kit. (Robert Vanderpool)

Japanese playing cards.

Magazines and Comics

The Gold Key *Space Family Robinson* comic predates the *Lost in Space* TV series by three years, starting in December 1962, having been created by writer Del Connell and artist Dan Spiegle. When Irwin Allen produced his series in 1965, Gold Key noticed the similarities with their comic book and considered filing a law suit against Allen. However, as Gold Key were already publishing an Irwin Allen title, *Voyage to the Bottom of the Sea*, they decided against this. Instead the two companies came to an arrangement with the comic changing its title to *Space Family Robinson: Lost in Space* starting with issue 15 in January 1966. While there are similarities none of the comic book stories actually feature any of the characters from the TV series, so these are only tenuously connected to the series, really only sharing the name *Lost in Space*. The title ultimately ceased publication after fifty-nine issues in 1982, having had several hiatuses during its run.

The series was featured in a *Mad* magazine satire in July 1966, issue 104. (UK edition issue 58.)

The show appeared on the cover of many TV listings magazines around the world. Some of the notable ones in the USA are the *Seattle Post Intelligencer TV Showtime* 3–9 September 1965, *Los Angeles Herald Examiner TV Weekly* 19–25 September 1965, *Cleveland Press TV Showtime Guide* 8–15 October 1965. *New York Journal American TV Magazine* 31 October–6 November 1965, *TV Guide* 6–12 November 1965, and *St Louis Post Dispatch TV Magazine* 10–16 December 1967.

TV Channels 3–9 October 1965. (Norman Fisher)

In Mexico it was featured on the cover of *TV Selecciones* dated 25 September 1966, and *Tele Guia* for the week of 28 December 1967–3 January 1968. The Chilean version of *Tele Guia* featured the series on the cover twice: the 1968 Christmas edition and 20 June 1969 edition. The *New Zealand TV Weekly* featured the series as its cover star on 3 June 1968.

While the show appears to have had only one *TV Guide* cover in the USA, the magazine did do several features on the series. The *TV Guide* dated 5–11 February 1966 carried a full-page review of the series, then the 18–24 June 1966 issue contained the feature 'One case where evil triumphs'. Guy Williams was featured in an interview for the 24–30 September 1966 issue, while the feature 'To make a Robot fly' was included in the 22–28 July 1967 issue. The Australian *TV Times* would feature a full-page colour photograph of Dr Smith and the Robot to promote the series in its 29 November 1966 issue.

Trading Cards and Miscellaneous

Various trading cards appeared globally. In the USA Topps Chewing Gum issued a set of fifty-five cards featuring black and white images from the TV series in 1966. A set also appeared in Spain. At least two of what are believed to be milk caps were produced in Argentina, which form part of a much larger set, around 1969, including stars of many different TV shows. It is possible that the set may have been an open-ended one, with new cards being added periodically. The two caps seen are No. 335, Prof. John Robinson, and No. 336, Major Don West. It is unknown if other characters from the series appeared. Caps are approximately 2 inches across and feature art by De Los Rios.

A dome-topped lunchbox was produced by King Seeley in 1967. While this came with a flask, only the lunchbox featured imagery from the TV series. The flask featured unrelated general space-type imagery. Beware, this was reproduced in the 1990s.

Topps trading cards.

Left: Album for Spanish trading card set. (Bernard Dunne)

Below: Spanish cards. (Bernard Dunne)

Right: Lunchbox and thermos. (Robert Vanderpool)

Below: Coca-Cola bottle tops. (Robert Vanderpool)

As a promotion for the Australian TV channel NWS-9 Coca-Cola bottle caps featuring images of John, Maureen, Don, Judy, Penny, and Will appeared. The poor-quality photographic images were revealed on the inside of the cap when removed from the bottle.

In Japan two record and storybook sets were issued by Asahi Sonorama. These look to be Japanese versions of read-a-long storybooks where you could follow the story in a book while listening along to the audio on either record or tape.

Above: Japanese record and storybook. (Bernard Dunne)

Left: Japanese record and storybook. (Bernard Dunne)

The Time Tunnel

The series is set in the near future (1968), and is based upon the exploits of Tony Newman (James Darren) and Doug Phillips (Robert Colbert), scientists involved with Project Tic Toc, a top-secret US Government-funded program researching time travel.

The Time Tunnel first aired on the ABC network in September 1966 with the episode 'Rendezvous with Yesterday'. In the first episode a budget-conscious senator is visiting the tunnel complex to assess where the $7.5 billion in taxpayers' money is being spent and with what progress. Seeing very little, he threatens to pull the plug upon his return to Washington. Later that night Tony takes matters into his own hands, entering the tunnel and losing himself in time. He arrives, unfortunately, aboard the *Titanic* only hours before its collision with an iceberg. This event gives the senator proof that time travel is possible and the project's funding is safe. Tony, however, is not, and therefore Doug enters the tunnel in an attempt to retrieve him. This attempt fails, with the tunnel controls only able to swap the two men from one time period to another, but unable to return them to the present.

This series is arguably the best one to have been made by Irwin Allen, though it was the least successful commercially, with only thirty hour-long episodes being made in its short run.

Products will normally have the copyright details '© Kent Productions – 20th Century Fox Film Corporation' on them.

Books/Annuals

It is noted that *Time Tunnel* by Murray Leinster first appeared from Pyramid Books two years prior to the TV series in 1964. It is unknown if this influenced the TV series, but it was Pyramid Books who, using the same writer, brought out *The Time Tunnel* based on the

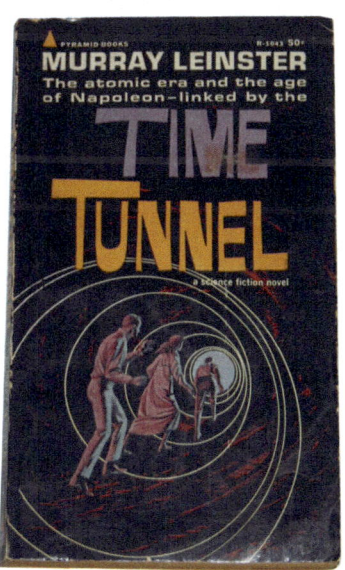

Non-TV series 1964 *Time Tunnel* book.

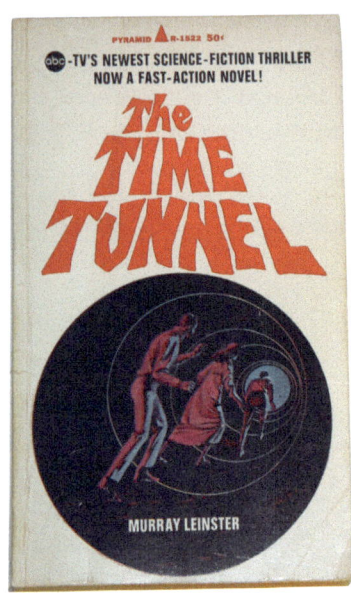

The Time Tunnel book's first and second covers.

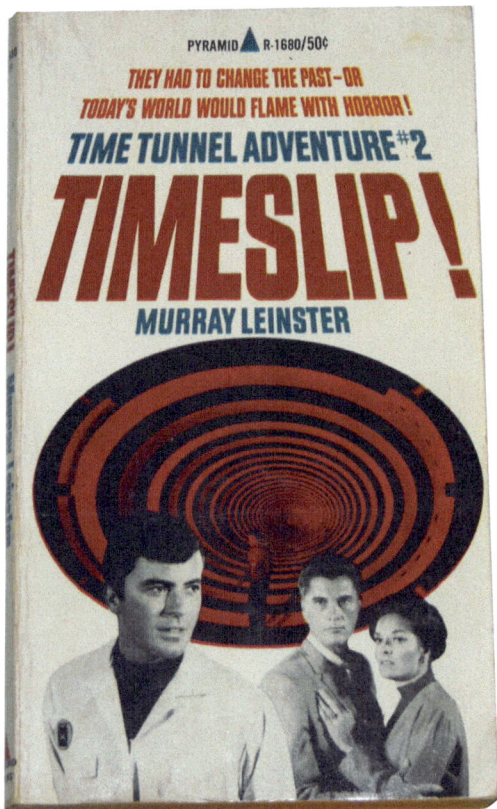

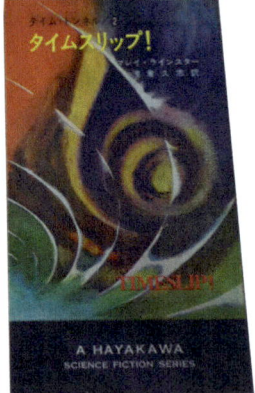

Above left: *Time Tunnel Adventure #2: Timeslip!* paperback.

Above right: Japanese *Time Tunnel* books 1 and 2, showing both cover and paper dust jacket of both. (Bernard Dunne)

Saalfield colouring book.

series in 1967, early copies having a very similar cover to the previous Pyramid publication with later covers changing to include a photograph from the series. Both of these editions claim to be a first printing. This also saw publication in Japan from Hayakawa-Shobo Co., as did Murray Leinster's second novel based on the series: *Time Tunnel Adventure #2: Timeslip!*, also from Pyramid Books in 1967. Both books had an original publication price of 50 cents. Interestingly both Doug and Tony are able to return to the tunnel complex at the end of these novels, unlike the TV series.

Saalfield brought out a colouring book for the series in 1967 at a cost of 29 cents.

Toys/Games

The board game for *The Time Tunnel* was produced by Ideal in 1966 and featured a playing board split into four different time zones. The winner was the first player able to successfully pass through all the zones. The box insert is nicely illustrated as the entrance to the Time Tunnel, having a pop-out spinner at its centre for controlling players' movements within the game.

Ideal also made a *Time Tunnel* card game in 1966, which came presented in a rather nice plastic case that contained the cards, a spinner and plastic counters. While cards are made to represent different time zones, it a simple game where the objective is to get rid of all of your cards.

Pressman produced a Spin to Win game in 1967. The game used small spinning tops on a board printed with black and white circles each representing a different time zone with a hole positioned in it. The winner would be the first player to spin their disc into a preselected time zone hole and then return to the present by further spinning their disc to the centre hole marked return. This is probably the hardest of the games to find.

Above and left: Ideal board games.

Above: Japanese *Time Tunnel* model kit. (Vectis)

Right: Reel set.

The only model kit for the series was produced in Japan by Fujimi in 1966. This plastic kit represented the tunnel control room and entrance, the tunnel forming a viewer through which supplied slides of historical periods could be viewed.

Sawyers produced View-Master set B491, which included a sixteen-page story booklet, for the series in 1966. The images for the set came from the series' first episode 'Rendezvous with Yesterday'. After Sawyers were taken over it was reissued with the GAF name on its packets. This second version is much scarcer than the original Sawyers issued sets.

Magazines/Comics

Gold Key produced two comics priced at 12 cents based upon the series. The first (in 1966) contained two stories: The Assassins and The Lion or the Volcano. The second (in 1967) contained The Conquerors and The Captives. Both saw publication in Mexico by Domingos Alegres.

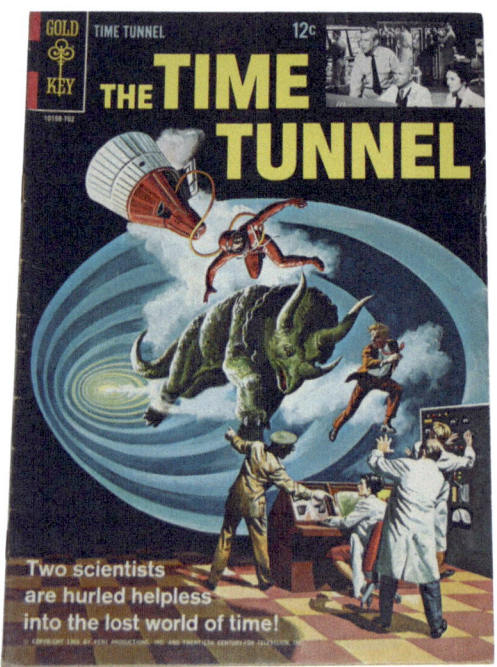 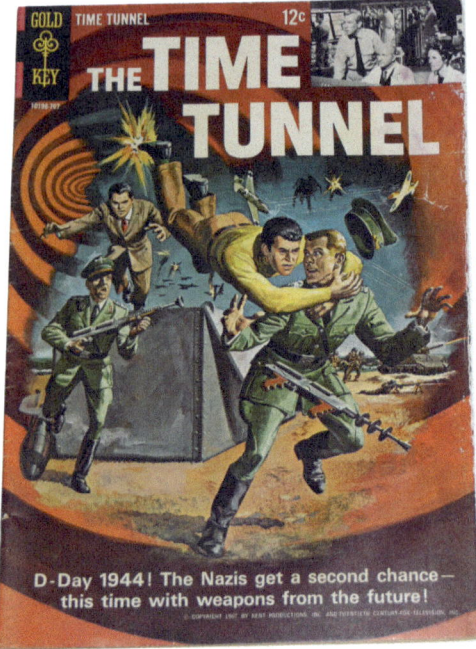

Gold Key comics.

Several TV listing magazines around the world featured covers for the series. Those noted include *St. Louis Globe-Democrat* 15–21 October 1966, *The Knickerbocker News TV Magazine* 22 October 1966, *Los Angeles Herald-Examiner* 26 February– 4 March 1967, in the USA. In Canada *The Telegram TV Weekly* 21–28 October 1966 featured the show on its cover. Other covers included *Canal TV* 4 July 1967 in Argentina, *Lecturas* 18 August 1967 in Spain, The *New Zealand TV Weekly* 16 September 1968, and *Teve Guia* 20–26 May 1967 in Purto Rico.

In the USA *TV Guide* carried features in at least three issues. The 10–16 September 1966 issue contained an introductory feature for the series, while the 10–16 June 1967 issue included a feature titled 'This way out'. Then the 24–30 June 1967 issue contained 'A teen-age idol passes 30', a feature and interview with James Darren.

Trading Cards and Miscellaneous

Four trading cards featuring colour photographs from the series were issued in the late sixties, by Monty Gum of Holland, forming part of a larger set covering several different series. While in Argentina two illustrated milk caps appeared as part of a larger set. Card No. 266 showed Doug, while Tony was on card No. 267.

In Japan Asahi Sonorama produced an illustrated storybook with a record in 1967. While a set of what the Japanese call bromides were produced for the show, these are almost postcard-sized trading cards, which came in packs from vending machines. There appear to be at least seventeen colour photographs with blank backs in the set.

The Hastings Music Corp published sheet music for the series, with a photographic cover, in 1966 at a price of 75 cents.

18. Time Tunnel

19. Time Tunnel

20. Time Tunnel

21. Time Tunnel

22. Time Tunnel

Dutch trading cards including card 18, which is wrongly titled as *The Time Tunnel* but actually shows an image from *Voyage to the Bottom of the Sea*. (Remco Admiraal)

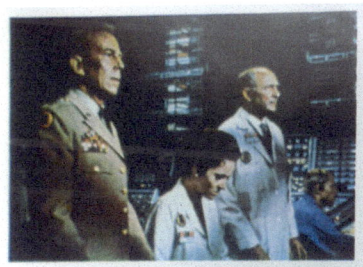

Japanese bromides. (Bernard Dunne)

Voyage to the Bottom of the Sea

Starting as a feature film in 1961, *Voyage* became a highly successful TV series, running for 110 episodes between 1964 and 1968. Both were based around the 400-foot-long atomic submarine *Seaview*, commanded by Admiral Harriman Nelson (Director of the Nelson Institute for Marine Research).

In the 20th Century Fox film, Admiral Nelson was played by veteran actor Walter Pidgeon, while Richard Basehart replaced him in the TV series. His second in command, Captain Lee Crane, was played by Robert Sterling (in the film), and then later David Hedison (in the series), who was also to play Felix Leiter in at least two of the Bond movies.

The film is a race against time story as the world faces global disaster. A ring of radiation around the earth has been set ablaze and unless extinguished the Earth's temperature will rise, causing the destruction of the planet. *Voyage to the Bottom of the Sea* was the runaway box office success of 1961, and Allen, eager to move into the lucrative world of television, suggested to American network ABC TV that it would be possible to develop the idea into a series. Many of the existing sets and models created for the film could be reused, enabling costs to be kept down.

The show's first season was produced in black and white, lasting for thirty-two episodes before converting to colour in its second season. As with all of Allen's TV series, this was set in the near future, with episodes giving dates between 1978 and 1980. The *Seaview*'s primary mission was marine research, though first season episodes extensively concern its use to defend the free world against saboteurs and enemy agents.

Later seasons tended to become slightly silly, with the *Seaview* being invaded by spacemen, robots, a werewolf and other equally unlikely situations and predicaments. One other introduction to the TV series was that of the Flying Sub. This was a high-tech combination aircraft/midget submarine, housed in a docking bay at the front of the *Seaview*.

Products will normally have the copyright details '© Cambridge Productions Inc.' on them.

Books/Annuals
Theodore Sturgeon novelised the movie version of *Voyage to the Bottom of the Sea* in 1961 for Pyramid Books. This was reissued with a photo cover for the TV series in 1964. Editions of this book also appeared in Dutch, German and Spanish, with two different editions appearing in Japanese.

A second novel appeared from Pyramid Books in April 1965. This one was called *City Under the Sea* and was written by Paul W. Fairman. This title also appears to have also been published in Spanish and Japanese.

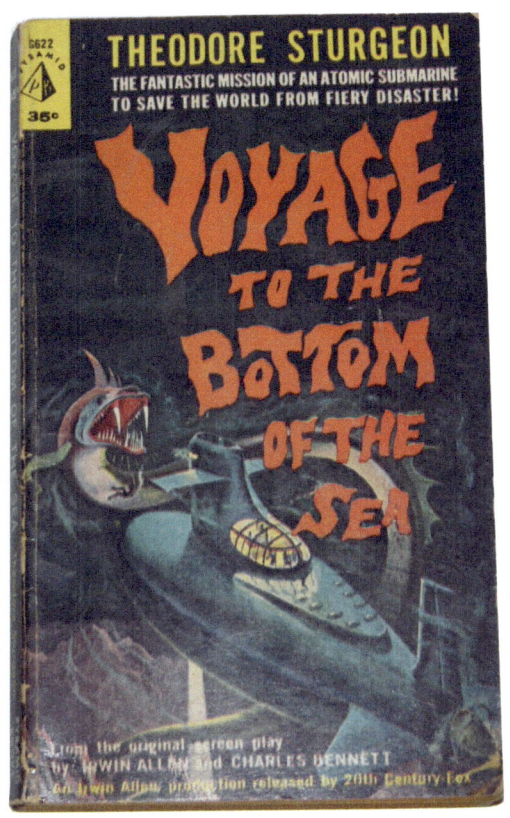
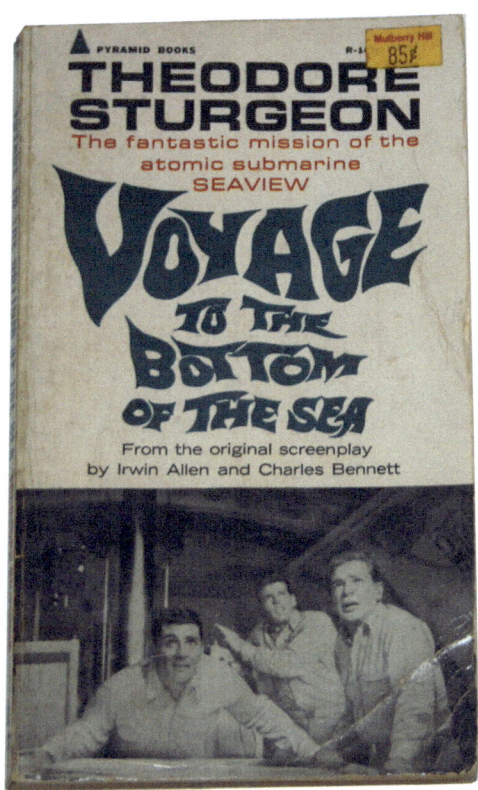

Above: Film novelisation first and second editions.

Right: Dutch film paperback. (Bernard Dunne)

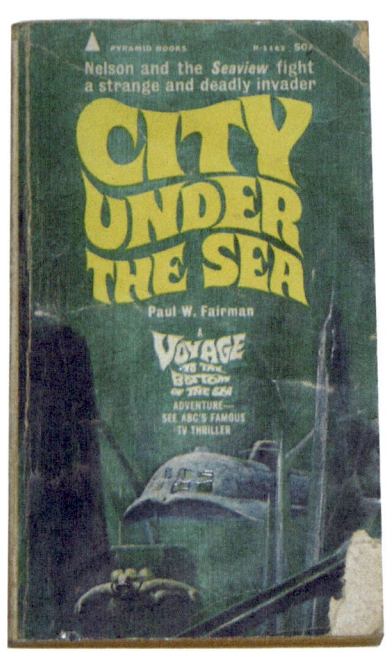

City Under the Sea UK and Spanish editions. (Bernard Dunne)

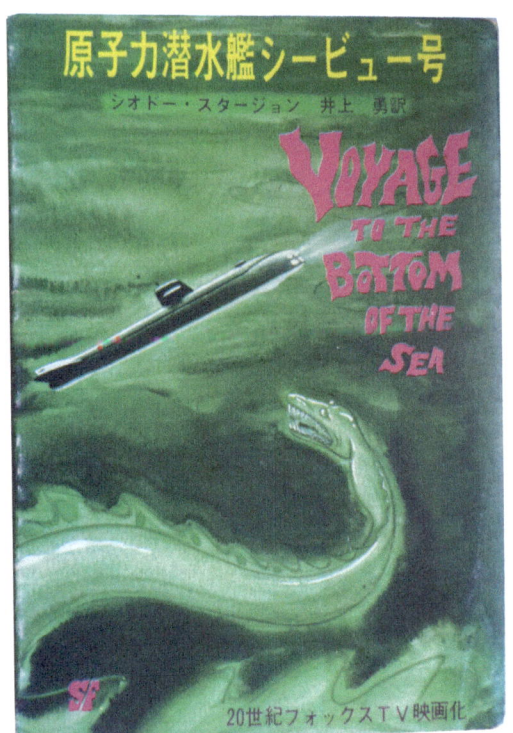
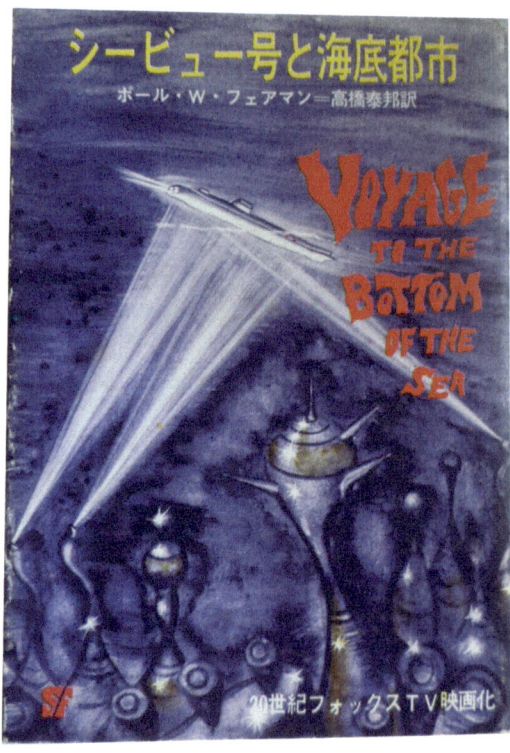

Above left: Japanese film paperback. (Bernard Dunne)

Above right: Japanese edition. (Bernard Dunne)

Two British annuals were published by World Distributors Ltd, the first coming out in 1966, with a second in 1967. Both annuals contained a mix of text and strip stories. The first annual (1966) has a photograph of Admiral Nelson, with a smaller insert photograph of Commander Crane, and an illustration of the *Seaview* at the bottom. The annual has a red spine. Stories included the 'Kingdom of Davy Jones', 'The Statue Maker' and 'Robinson Crusoe of the Depths'.

The second annual (1967) has a green/blue cover with a large central illustration of the *Seaview*. Above this is a photograph of Commander Crane, while a photo of Admiral Nelson is below. The spine for this annual is white. Stories included 'Ten Thousand Feet of Ice', 'Rock of Terror' and 'The Great Undersea Safari'. Both annuals had a publication price of 10s 6d.

World Distributors also produced the *Voyage to the Bottom of the Sea Comic Album No. 1* in 1965 at a publication price of 2s 6d. This contained reprints from the Gold Key-produced comics.

In the Netherlands a soft covered annual was published using the cover from the first of the two British annuals, while in the USA a colouring book was published by Watkins Strathmore for the series in 1965, containing line drawing by Jason Studios. Also in the USA a hardback storybook was produced by Whitman Publishing in 1964. This was written by Raymond F. Jones and contained illustrations by Leon Jason Studios.

Several Spanish storybooks were produced. The first appears to contain translated reprints of the Gold Key comics, which was published by Laida, while a second appears to

Above left: UK Annual 1966.

Above right: UK Annual 1967.

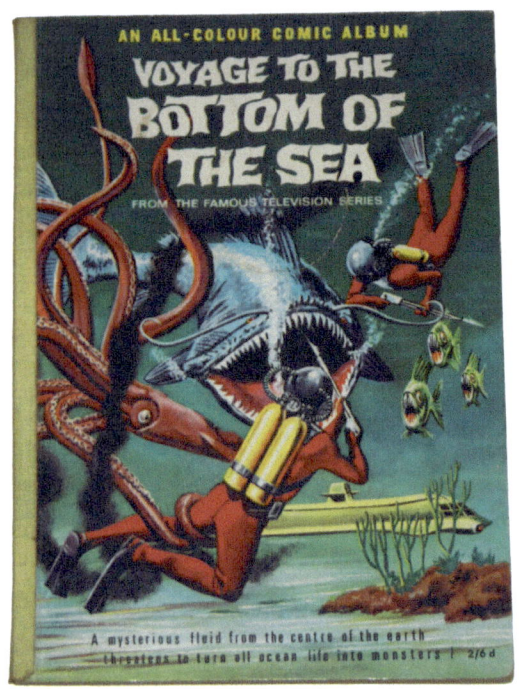

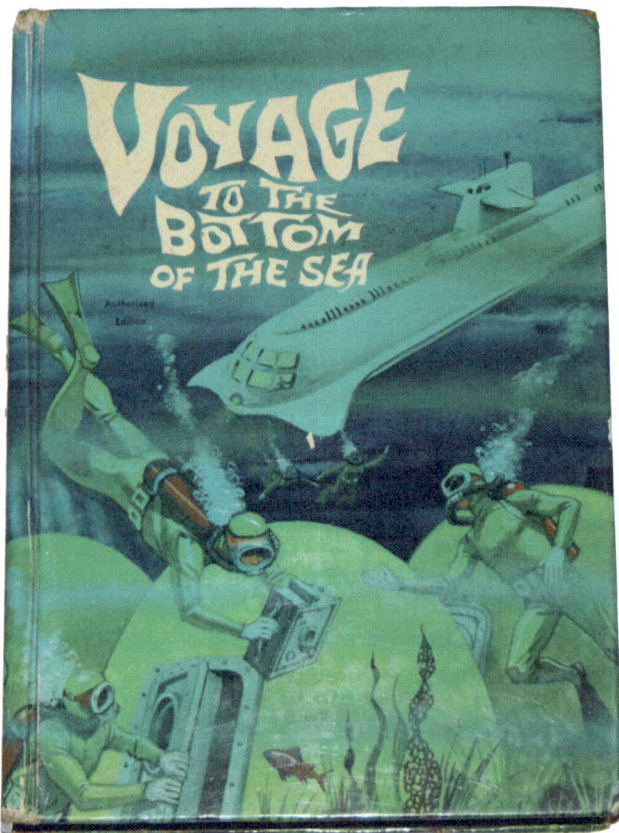

Above left: Comic Album No. 1.

Above right: Colouring book.

Left: Whitman hardback.

Spanish storybook.

be text stories translated from the British annuals, which was published by Fher. Publishers Editorial Bruguera. S. A. also produced at least four storybooks for the series that were similar in format to those produced by the firm for *Land of the Giants*.

In the UK, the series featured in three *TV Tornado* annuals published by World Distributors Ltd. The 1967 annual, priced at 10s 6d, contained the text story 'Terror of the Deep'. The 1969 annual saw the *Seaview* featuring on the cover as part of a montage of different series. The *Seaview* also featured as the inside cover illustration. Two stories featured in this annual: a text story, 'The Children of Neptune', and a strip story, 'City under the Sea'. Both this and the 1970 *TV Tornado* annual had a publication price of 12s 6d. The 1970 annual again featured the *Seaview* in a montage of different series upon its cover, and it also contained both a text story, 'Menace from the Mindanao', and a strip story, 'Neptunius the Fish Man'.

The Spanish publishers Ediciones Este in 1964, as issue 13 in their *Figuras de la T.V. – Biografia lustrada* series, produced *David Hedison Y Richard Basehart, en Viaje al Fondo Del Mar*, which included biographies of both stars of the series.

Above left: Spanish storybook.

Above right: Spanish storybook *El Navio Fantasma*. (Bernard Dunne)

Left: Spanish storybook *La Isla de Metal*. (Bernard Dunne)

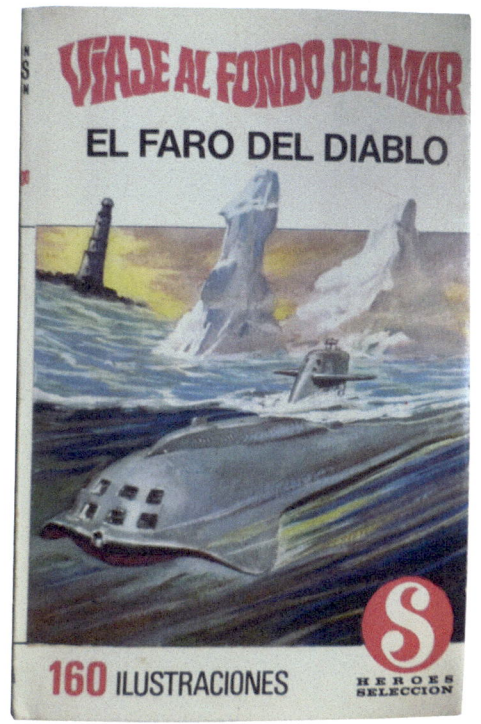

Above left: Spanish storybook *El Faro Del Diablo*. (Bernard Dunne)

Above right: Spanish storybook *La Isla Maldita*. (Bernard Dunne)

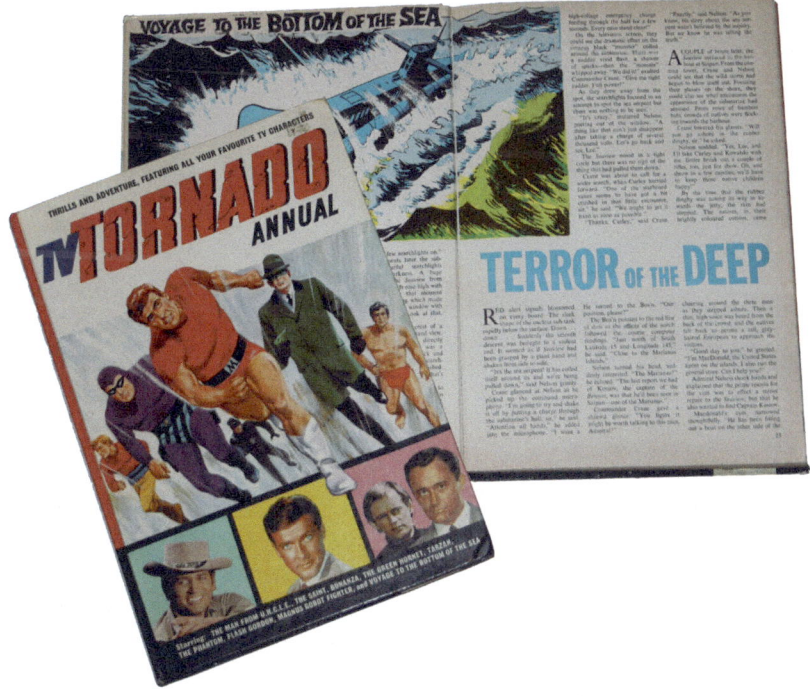

TV Tornado Annual 1967.

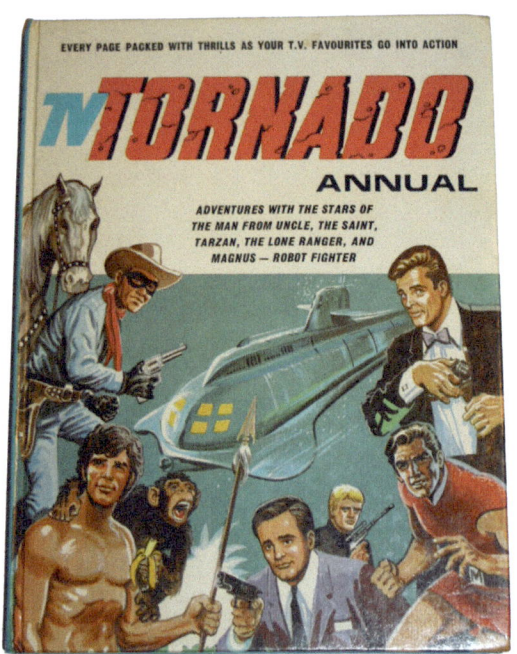

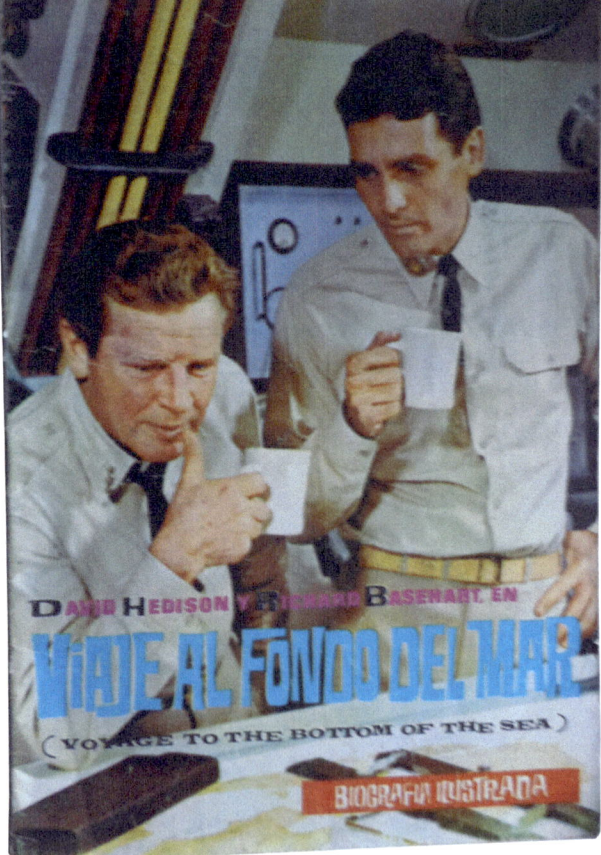

Above left: TV Tornado Annual 1969.

Above right: TV Tornado Annual 1970.

Left: Spanish biographic book. (Bernard Dunne)

Toys

A board game based upon the movie was promoted in the exhibitor's campaign book for the film in 1961. This apparently was produced by the firm Gem Color and was to have sold for $2.

While no examples of this film-based game seem to have appeared on collectors' circuits, the Milton Bradley game, based on the TV series in 1964, does quite often. This featured an illustrated box lid showing a car crashing through the barrier of a coastal road, with two motorbikes in pursuit. A helicopter is hovering overhead, with its passenger brandishing a machine gun. The *Seaview* is below this, having fired a missile, which is about to hit the helicopter. The object of this two-player game is to capture all of your opponent's submarines. The game comes with sixteen card discs representing submarines, eight blue with a white sub and eight red with a black sub. The board is nicely illustrated with various nautical themes around its edge, while the box inlay is a slightly poorer-quality printing of some of these scenes, with a spinner to determine player moves.

Above: Color Gem board game advert from movie press book.

Below: Milton Bradley board game.

Left: Milton Bradley/John Sands board game comparison. (Craig Nobes)

Below: Milton Bradley card game.

Junior jigsaws. (Craig Nobes)

More products were to appear from Milton Bradley including a card game, two different junior jigsaws, and a boxed set of four tray puzzles All of these products saw an Australian issue by John Sands. The first of the two junior puzzles used the same artwork that had been used upon the board game's lid. This artwork was further reused as one of the frame puzzles. The second puzzle depicts a giant octopus with frogmen trapped in its tentacles and the *Seaview* in the background. This design was again used for one of the tray puzzles. The third of the frame puzzles depicted a shark attacking frogmen, while the final puzzle once again had a giant octopus, this time wrapped around the wreck of a tall ship, with an undersea base in foreground and the *Seaview* behind.

Whitman also produced a 100-piece junior jigsaw puzzle in 1964, which showed Admiral Nelson and Commander Crane in the control room of the Seaview with a frogman visible through the observation window.

Sawyers View-Master set B 483, produced in 1964, took the standard format of three reels and a sixteen-page story booklet. A second issue of the set sees the Sawyers logo replaced by GAF on packets. Photographs for the set from the episode 'Deadly Creature Below' featured. GAF also produced a Tru-Vue Magic Eyes set in 1966 using the same images.

Aurora produced two model kits based on the series. The first kit, No. 707, was a fairly accurate representation of the *Seaview* as seen in both the movie and first season of the TV show. This kit can be found in two sizes of box: both boxes carry the same artwork but

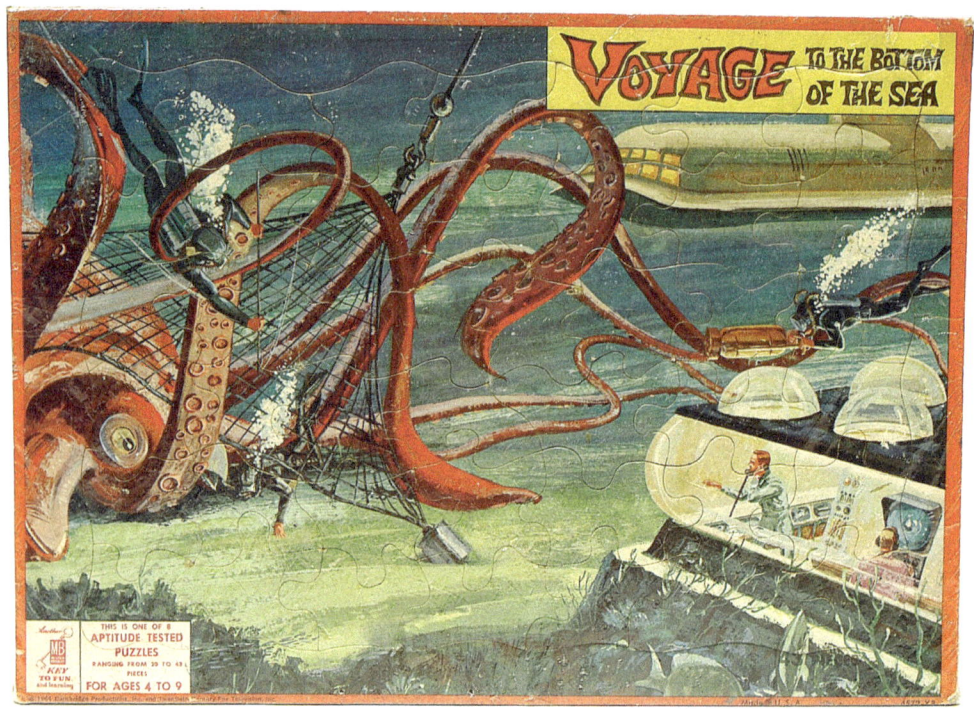

Tray puzzle. (Vectis)

Tray puzzle. (Robert Vanderpool)

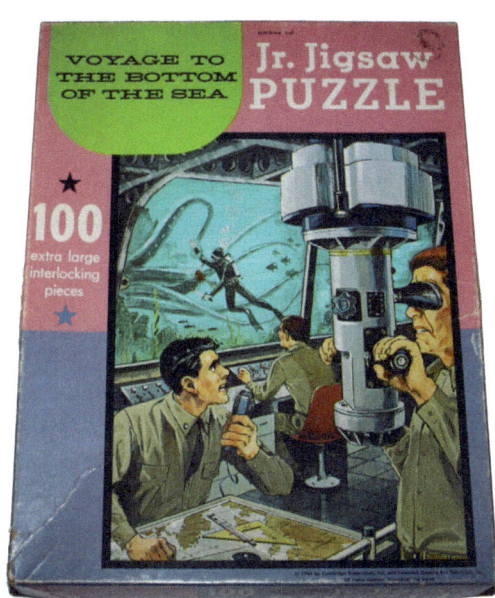

Right: Whitman jigsaw.

Below: View-Master set

Tru-Vue Magic Eye set.

one is longer than the other. The longer box is possibly from slightly later in the production run as the kit fits better into this slightly longer-shaped box. A variation noted on the short box is the kit number: some show 707-100 and others 707-130. The kit was reissued by Aurora in a different-style box in the mid-seventies, before later reissues by Monogram, who took over the Aurora moulds in around 1977.

The second kit to be produced by Aurora was that of the flying sub, which was introduced in the TV series' second season. The model Aurora 817 saw release in 1968 and featured a removable top, enabling you to see the ship's interior. This too was reissued with different box art in the mid-seventies.

Several different play sets were produced by Remco in the sixties for *Voyage to the Bottom of the Sea*. The *Seaview* in these sets was based on the eight-window design used in the first season and for the most part the sets all came in what Remco describe as their Clear Vue Armor boxes or Big 'V' for short. These were window display boxes that showcased the models contained in a dramatic scene. These original white boxes do have a tendency to discolour over the years, turning almost a light tan colour, so beware if a box seems a little too white.

The first set from Remco in 1965 were set No. 649, which featured a yellow plastic 17-inch-long model of the *Seaview*. This was the standard model that would appear in almost every set form them. According to instructions supplied it was able to dive and surface like a real submarine and could be propelled along by an elastic band motor. It

Above: Aurora *Seaview* model kit short box.

Right: Aurora flying sub model kit. (Norman Fisher)

Remco *Seaview* (Stuart McKell)

Left: Remco mini sled and crawler. (Stuart McKell)

Below: Sears catalogue advert.

was also able to fire small plastic torpedoes, two of which were supplied and could clip to a carrying location on the vessel's hull. Included with the set were two deep-sea divers.

The next set from the company and the only one not to contain the *Seaview* was set No. 650, the submarine scout set. This set consisted of a 6½-inch-long mini-sled and a 9½-inch sea crawler, both in plastic. The sled is yellow with a blue-tinted dome over a pair of small plastic men. The sea crawler is yellow and metallic blue and holds two men and a silver control panel. Each item has a mini-sled or sea crawler sticker on its side and the set includes a small metallic blue treasure chest.

Set No. 647, the submarine explorer set, the last and largest set to appear in a Big 'V' box, contained all the contents of the previous two sets in one. This set was also sold through Sears catalogues. The Sears sets came in a plain mailer box with the company name and 'Fragile' written upon the side. A version of this set was sold through Mongomery Wards in 1967. This edition comes in a white carton box, printed with the show's title and detailing the contents.

The largest of the Remco sets was set No. 662. This set appears in two versions, both of which were Sears catalogue exclusives. This set again contained everything that had been in the first two sets. The sled and sea crawler in this set had clear domes though, not blue tinted. The additional items in the set were an 11-inch-wide vacuum-formed octopus and a solid moulded 6-inch-sized bug, a repainted item from the Hamilton's Invaders sets produced by the firm. Both of these items are extremely fragile and rare to find. This version was expanded the following year, again as a Sears exclusive, with the addition of a 10-inch-long hard plastic 'killer whale'. The domes on the sled and sea crawler also appear to have reverted to being blue tinted in these later sets.

In 1967 set No. 679 was issued by Remco. The sea crawler and mini-sled were both missing in this set, but all other items remained present, and it did see an improvement to the bug – no longer a solid plastic piece, this new all-yellow version has a scuttling action and sting-operated features. Also for some reason the sub's torpedoes are now in a silver plastic, previous versions being the same colour as the sub. This came in a carton box with a photographic label. This set also appeared as a Sears version, the only difference being the box, which for Sears was a plain white carton showing only the product number.

Remco also produced the incredibly rare four-way sub gun set. This futuristic-looking gun came with interchangeable barrels and plastic rockets. Produced in white and red plastic, it could be assembled as a bazooka gun, submarine gun, Tommy gun or a torpedo gun.

Magazines/Comics

In the USA Dell produced a comic book adaptation of the movie in 1961, with artwork by Sam Glanzman, while in Italy a different approach was taken in adapting the movie. The Italian comic was instead a photo novel comic, using over 200 black and white images from the feature film in its pages.

When the TV series appeared in 1964, Gold Key would produce a sixteen-issue run based on the new series. Issues were priced at 12 cents each, and this run started in December of 1964 with 'The Last Survivor'. Issues were somewhat sporadic. Issue 2 'Monsters of the Moho' did not appear until July 1965. Then issue 3 'The Jonah Cruise of the Seaview' appeared in October. May 1966 saw issue 4 with 'Robinson Crusoe of the Depths'. Then August saw 'The Great Undersea Safari'. November 1966 brought us 'The Overland Trail' in issue 6. Issue 7 appeared in February 1967 with 'Saga of the Undersea Island', and issue 8 contained 'Expedition to Doomsday' in May. This was followed in August with 'Seaview vs. the Ultra-sub', while November brought us 'Davy Jones' Locker'. Issue 11 appeared in February of 1968 containing 'S.O.S. Seaview', then issue 12 featured 'The Emperor of the Oceans' in May. 'The Renegade Island' appeared in the August issue. The last original story was 'The Life and Death of Seaview', which appeared in issue 14, November 1968. This issue

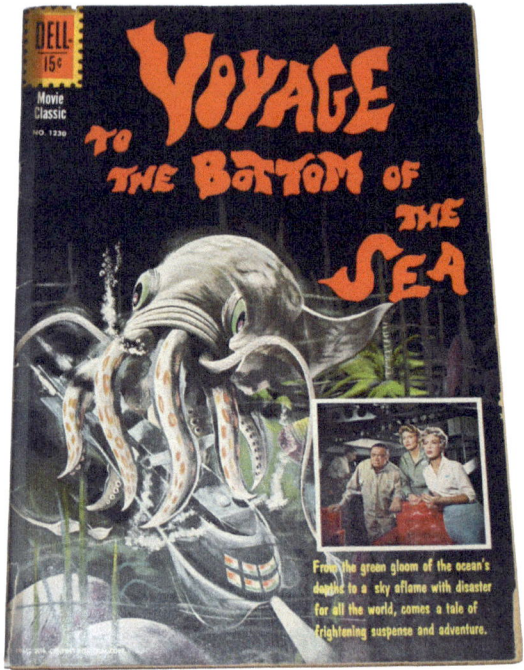 

Above left: Dell comic based on the movie.

Above right: Italian comic based on the movie.

also saw a price increase to 15 cents. Issue 15 in June 1969 reprinted issue 7, while the last issue, 16, in April 1970, was a reprint of issue 6.

In Mexico Domingos Alegres reprinted the Gold Key series of comics, and at least four issues of the Gold Key comic were reprinted in black and white for the Australian market. Similarly at least three issues also appeared as reprints in Germany.

In 1971 *Look-in* comic in the UK featured *Voyage to the Bottom of the Sea* as a very short-lived weekly strip story, running for only eight issues between 22 May, issue 20, and 10 July, issue 27.

The first sixteen issues of the City Magazines published *TV Tornado* comic featured *Voyage to the Bottom of the Sea* as a regular feature, starting in issue one as a two-page strip story before becoming text stories with issue 7, the page count also increasing to three pages an issue in No. 11. The series featured on the cover of five issues as part of montages of different shows. After issue 16, the show disappeared from the comic save for issue 22, which included a very small piece on Richard Basehart, and the cover to issue 54 (with a tiny inside piece about the star).

A French comic, *Vedettes TV*, featured the series, and the show appeared on the cover for issue 10. The series was satirised in the March 1966 issue of *Mad* magazine, issue 101 (*Mad* UK edition 54).

Both *TV Guide* 19–25 June 1965 and *New York Journal American TV Magazine* 30 January–5 February 1966 featured the series upon their covers in the USA. *New Zealand TV Weekly* featured the series upon its cover twice, on 5 December 1966 and 30 October

Gold Key No. 1.

1967, respectively. In Mexico the series featured on the cover of *Tele Guia* 23–29 September 1965.

In the 30 January–5 February issue of *TV Guide* a feature 'Down to the Sea in a Hollywood Moat', about making the series appeared. Then in the 1–7 May issue a full-page review of the series featured. A further feature 'Making the Seaview Scene' appeared in the 22–28 May 1965 issue.

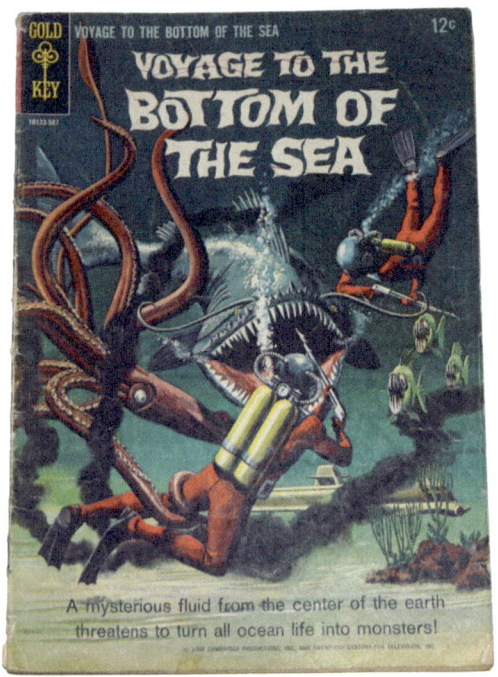
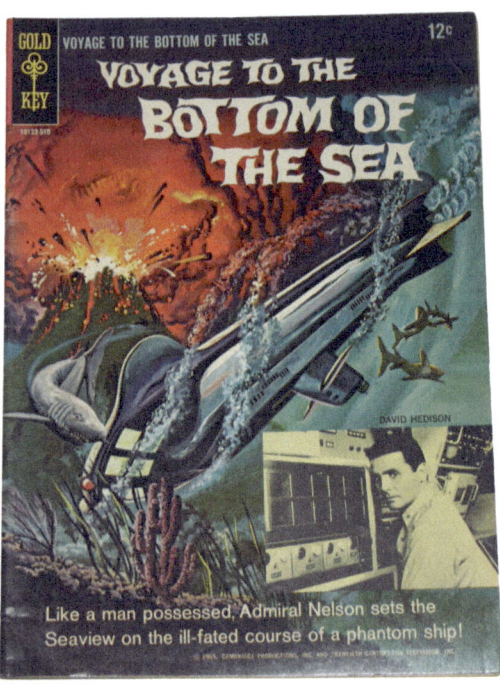
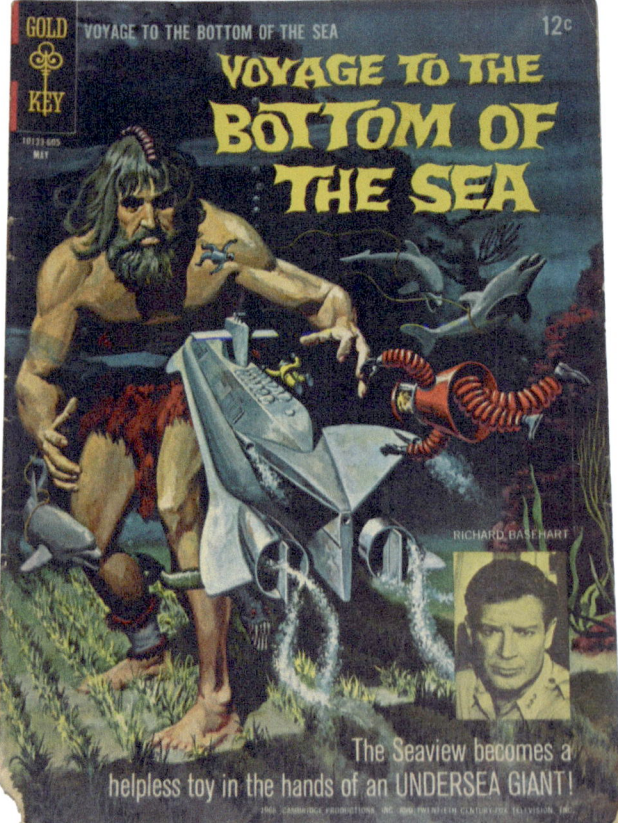

Above left: Gold Key No. 2.

Above right: Gold Key No. 3.

Left: Gold Key No. 4.

Gold Key No. 5.

Gold Key No. 6.

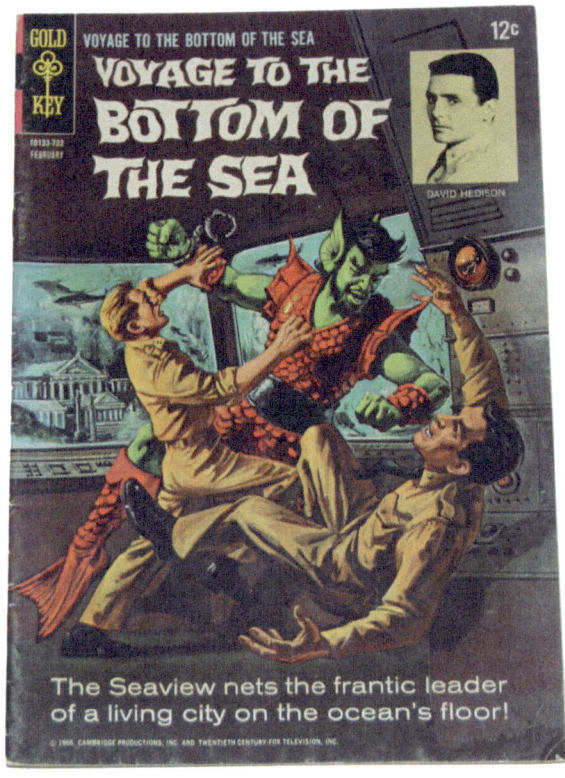

Gold Key No. 7.

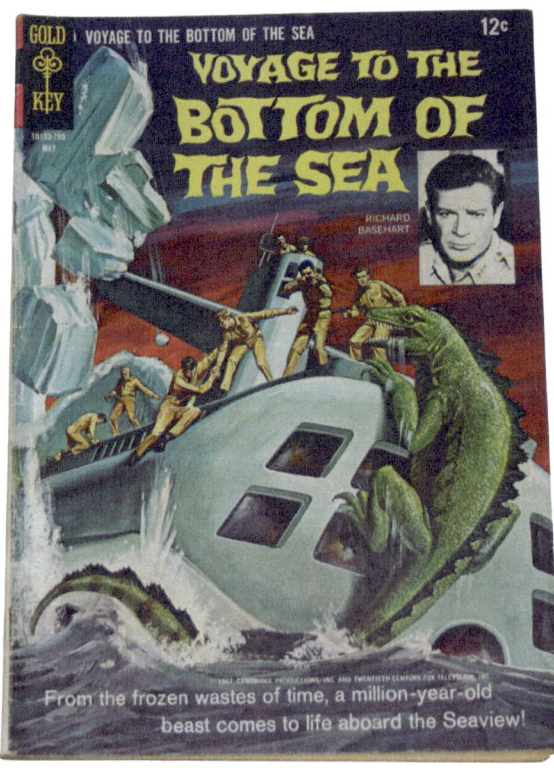

Gold Key No. 8.

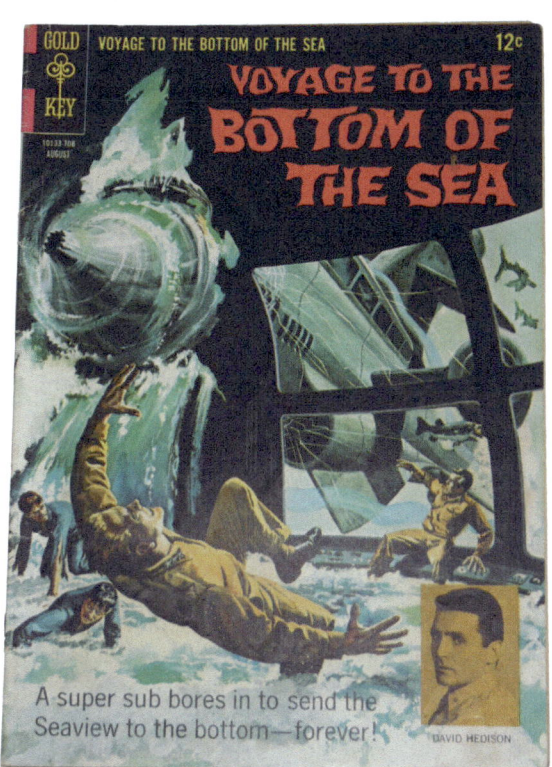

Gold Key No. 9.

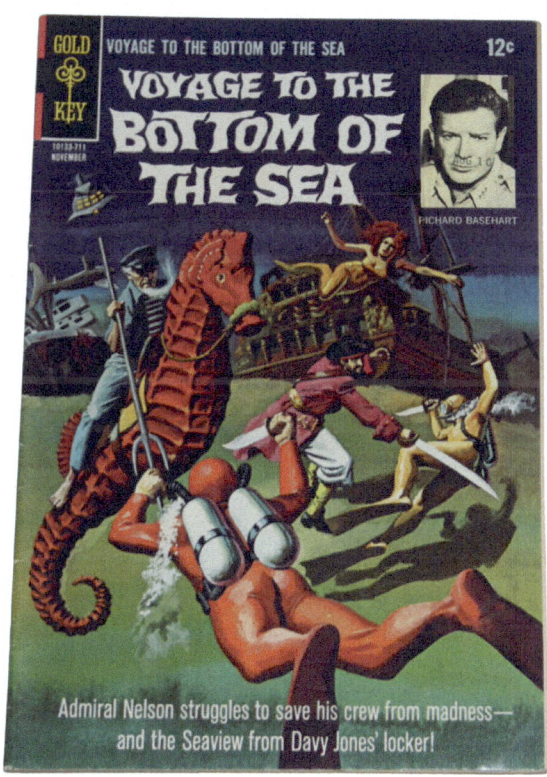

Gold Key No. 10.

81

Gold Key No. 11.

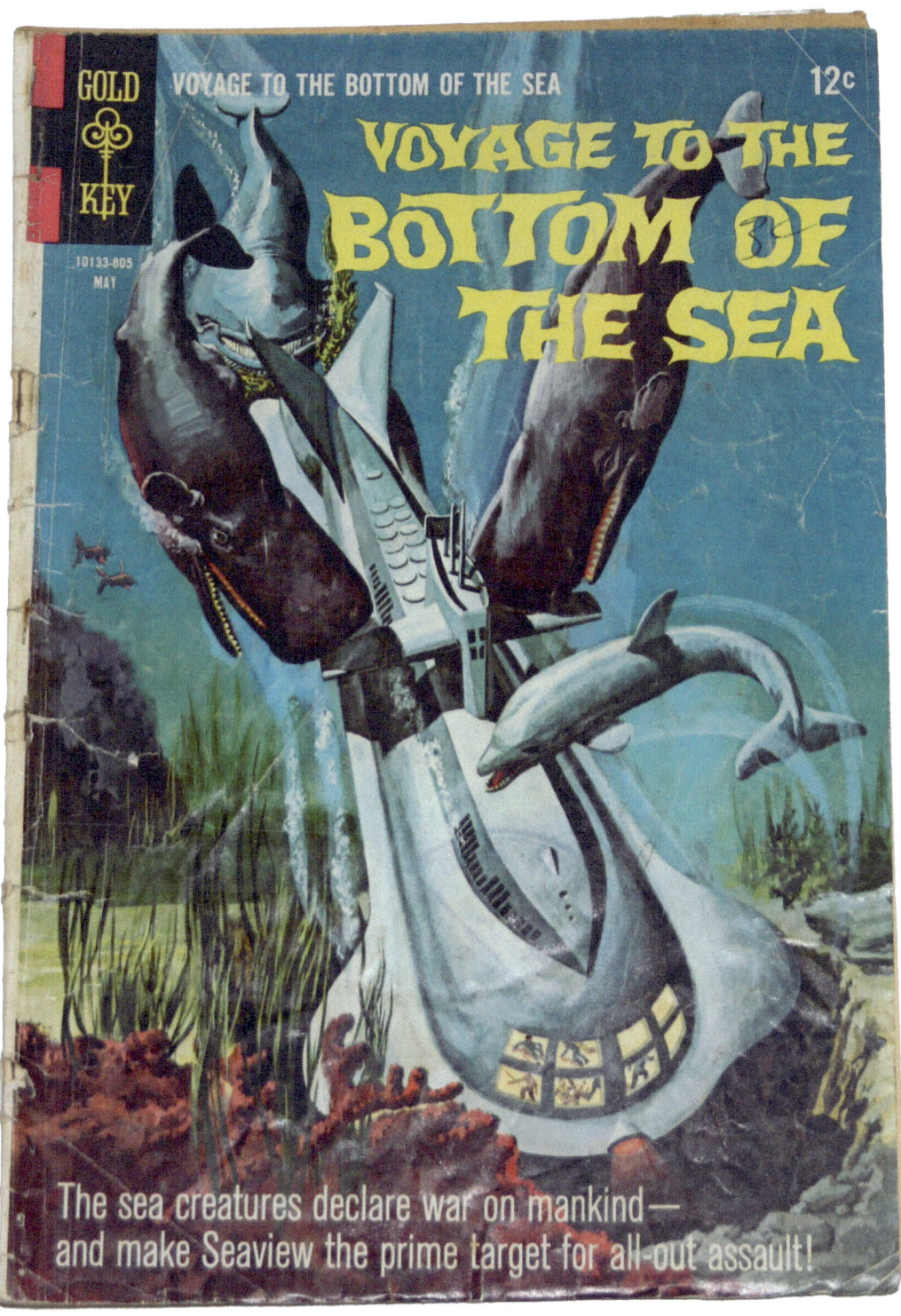

Gold Key No. 12.

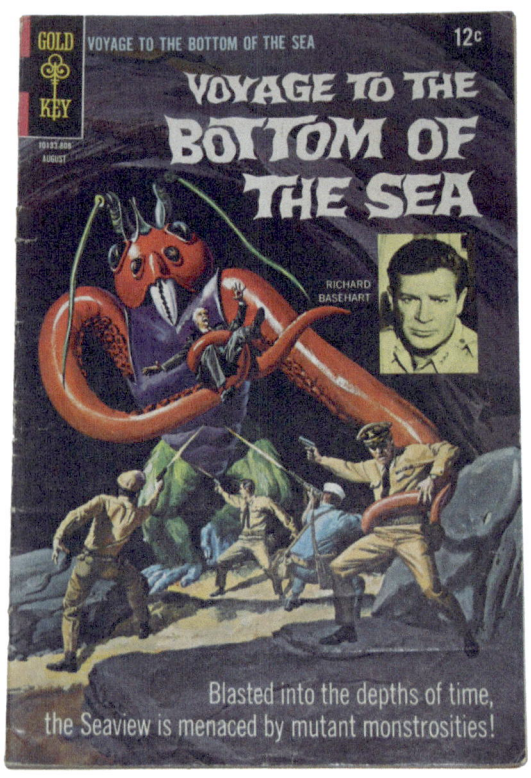

Gold Key No. 13.

Gold Key No. 14.

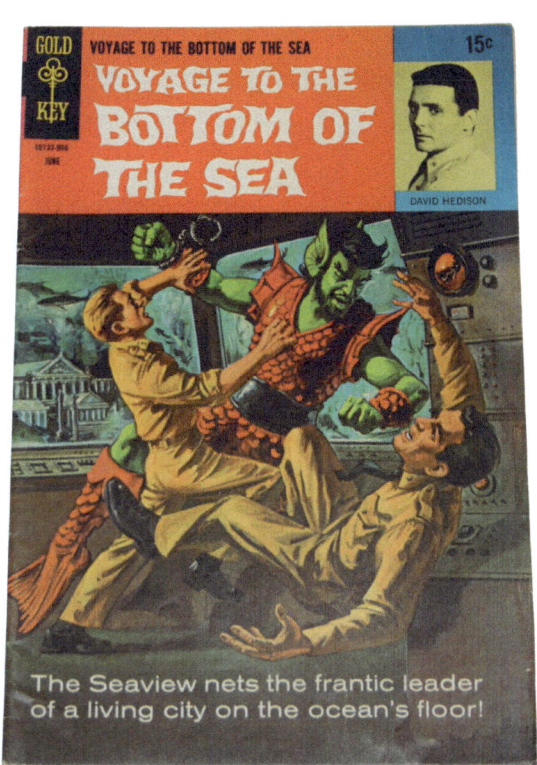

Gold Key No. 15.

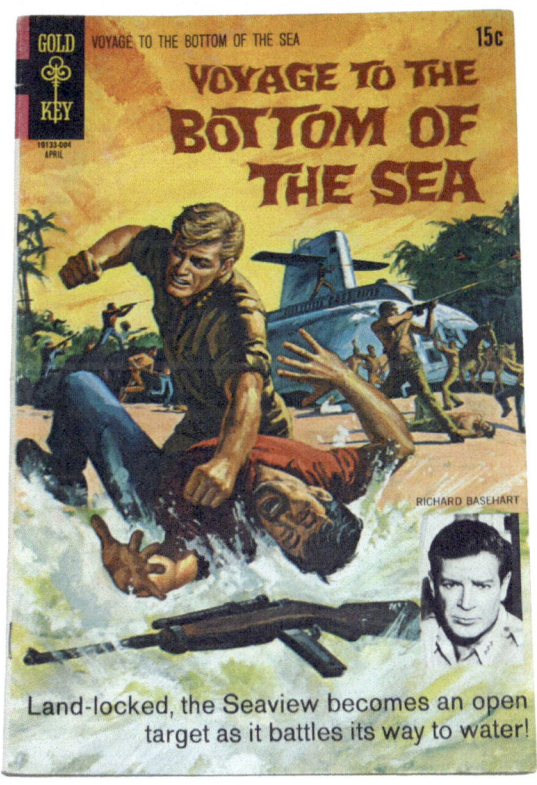

Gold Key No. 16.

Left: Dutch comic. (Remco Admiraal)

Below: French comics. (Bernard Dunne)

Look-in comics 1971.

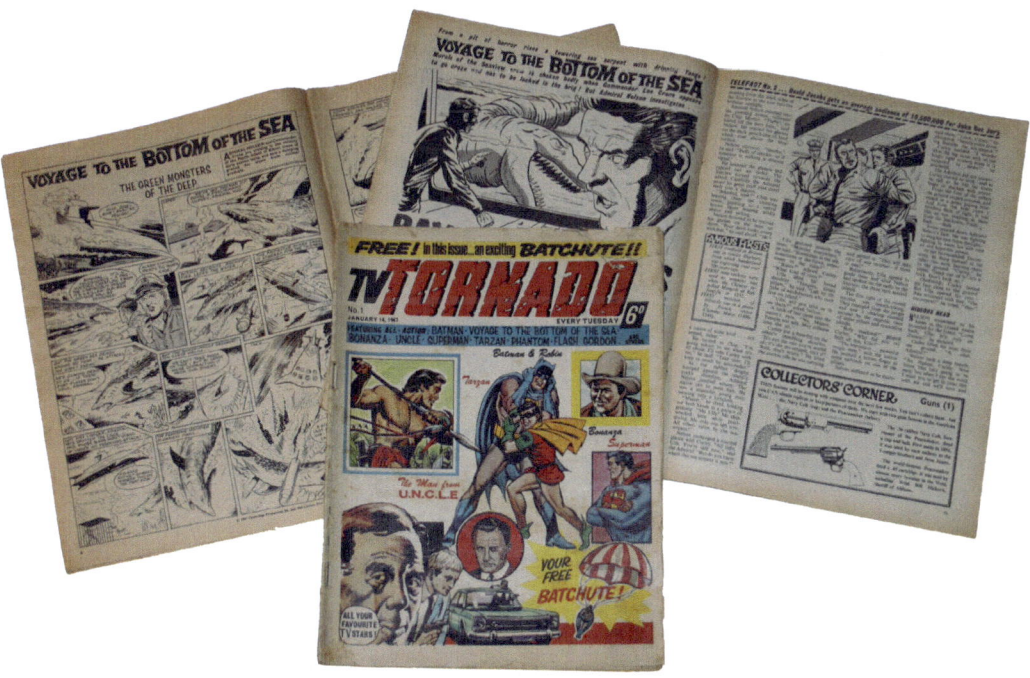

TV Tornado comics.

Left: *TV Tornado* No. 54.

Below: *TV Tornado* covers featuring *Voyage to the Bottom of the Sea*.

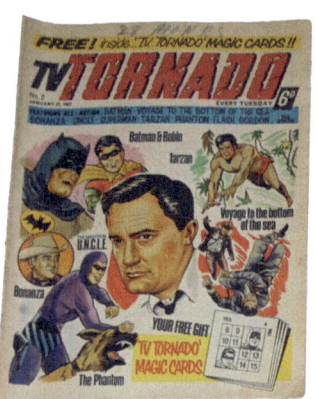
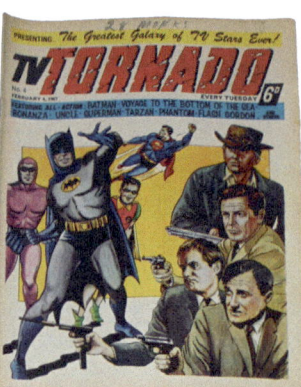

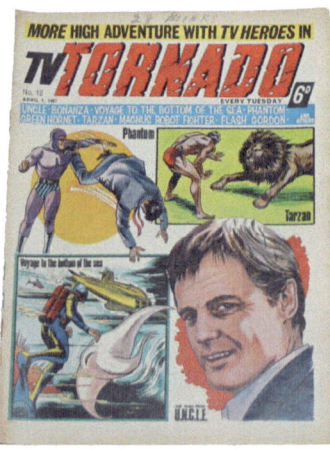
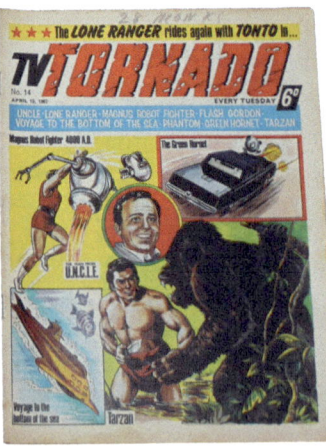

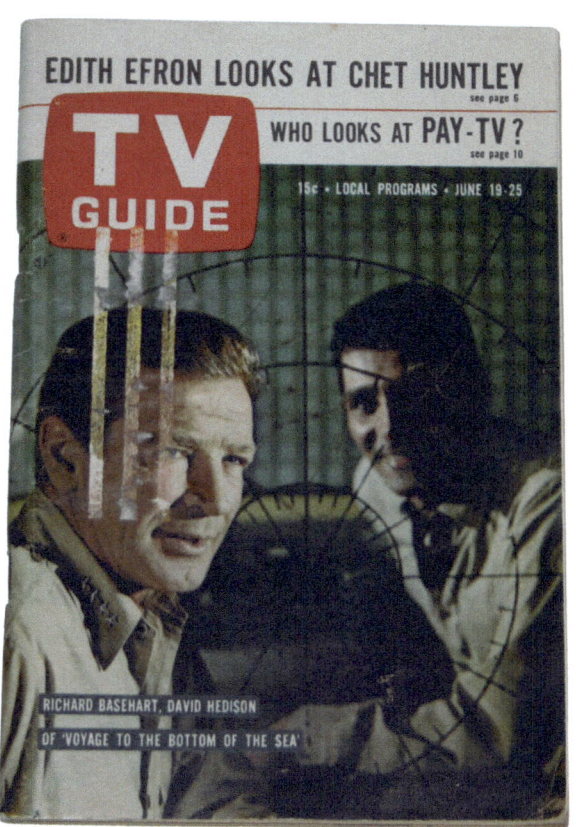

USA *TV Guide*.

Trading Cards and Miscellaneous

A set of sixty-six cards by Donruss were released in 1964. The cards feature black and white photographs from the series. The printing on the backs of the original-issue cards is blue. On the later reissue sets, the backs are printed in black. The cards in the reissue set are also slightly smaller than the originals. This reissue set dates from the early nineties and is not a late sixties European reissue as some unscrupulous dealers have claimed.

Monty Gum in the Netherlands produced three cards featuring the series as part of larger set. These were colour photographs with a blank back. Note: one of the cards was wrongly captioned as being Time Tunnel (Card 18). Also appearing in the Netherlands was a set of cigar bands from the firm Rokende Jan.

A super 360-foot reel of a 8-mm colour movie (with sound) featuring a seventeen-minute-long version of the 1961 movie was issued. Then silent 8-mm home movies of the show were released on 200-foot reels. These were released by Americom and came with a record of the soundtrack to play when viewing the film. Four titles appeared like this: The Atomic Cloud (two different-style boxes have been seen for this title), The Frogman, Sea of Mines, and The Octopus.

Aladdin Industries produced a lunchbox and flask for the series in 1967. One side featured the *Seaview* and a giant octopus, while the other side featured Admiral Nelson and Commander Crane viewing the octopus upon a screen. The flask featured an image of the *Seaview* and octopus.

Donruss unopened card pack. (Norman Fisher)

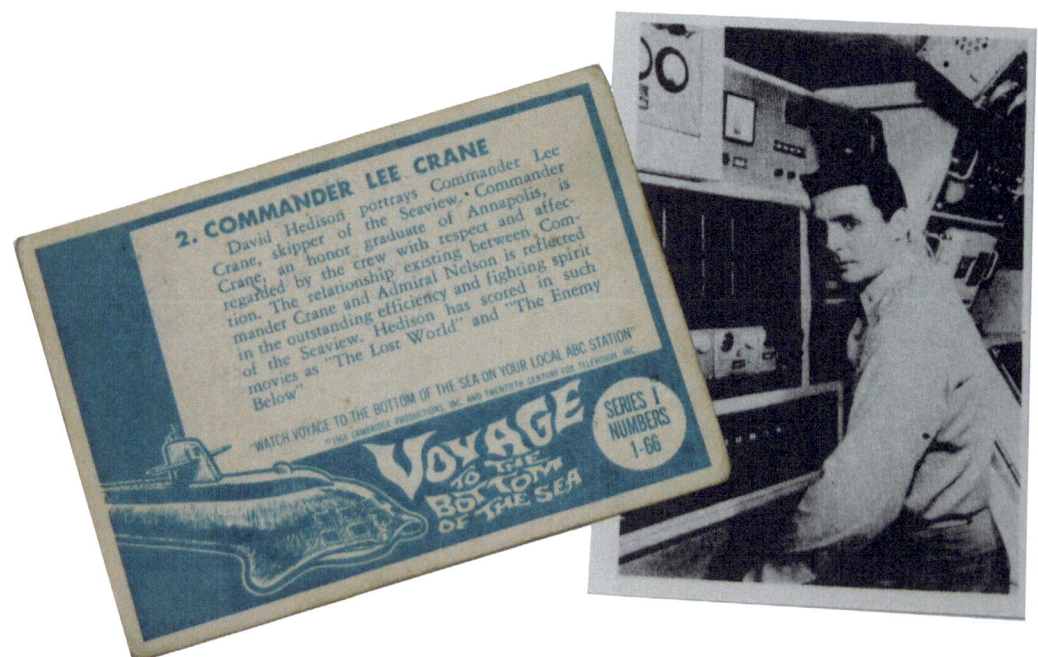

Donruss gum cards.

Spanish card album. (Bernard Dunne)

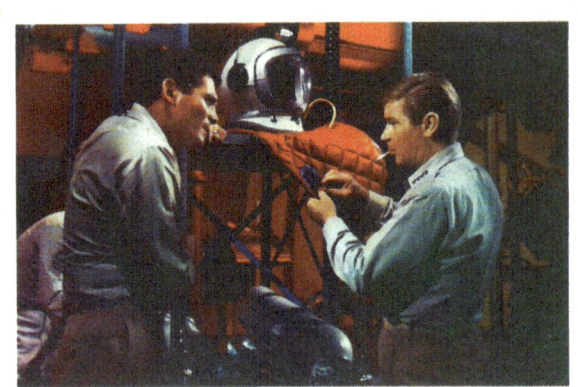

24. Voyage to Bottom of Sea

23. Voyage to Bottom of Sea

Monty Gum cards. (Remco Admiraal)

Cigar bands. (Remco Admiraal)

While this book has predominantly concentrated on products released for the TV series, there are a wealth of different styles of movie posters from the film version of *Voyage to the Bottom of the Sea* that were released around the world. Also among other items released were a picture sleeve single of the movie theme sung by Frankie Avalon. This was on the Chancellor label, and the sheet music saw several issues, both for the movie and TV release.

8-mm film highlights of the movie. (Norman Fisher)

Two different editions of the 8-mm film with record The Atomic Cloud. (Norman Fisher)

Above left: The Octopus 8-mm film with record. (Norman Fisher)

Above right: Sea of Mines 8-mm film with record. (Norman Fisher)

Left: The Frogman 8-mm film with record. (Norman Fisher)

Lunchbox side A. (Robert Vanderpool)

Lunchbox side B. (Robert Vanderpool)

Theme single picture sleeve.

Italian movie poster.

Acknowledgements

I would like to thank the following for their assistance in the preparation of this book:

Louise Harker at Vectis Toy Auctions, Remco Admiraal, Bernard Dunne, Stuart James McKell, Paul Gleave, Norman Fisher, Craig Nobes, and Robert Vanderpool (aka uncleodiescollectibles.com). Also thanks to the Little Storping Museum website, www.murdersville.co.uk/museum. Finally thanks to William Woodward for his help and proofreading skills.